"*Related by Chance, Family by Ch* ...tionships with biblical percep... persuades that 'in-law' relations... You will profoundly benefit from her keen insight into the Scriptures and her down-to-earth illustrations and practical life applications."
—**Laurie Dodds**, Speaker and author

"This book is a godsend of encouragement. . . . Every mother of a grown son, and every woman who marries a man with a mama, needs this book. I'm thankful someone had the wisdom and courage to write it!"
—**Becky Johnson**, Author of over 40 books, including *We Laugh, We Cry, We Cook*

"*Related by Chance, Family by Choice* is a must-read for anyone navigating the sometimes complex path of the relationship between a mother-in-law and her daughter-in-law. Deb DeArmond provides not only expert advice from personal experience, but she also provides tools, checklists, and action steps that one can take to make sure that this relationship is the best possible. I applaud this important work!"
—**Susan Steinbrecher**, Founder of Heart Centered Leadership

"Deb's book is original and fresh—full of excellent insights, tips, and probing exercises that encourage you to consider the perspective of your own 'woman-in-law.' I love the fact that it exposes the world's view of the 'in-law' mentality and emphasizes how to build stronger, more loving relationships with your 'in-loves.'"
—**Carol Doyer**, Editor-in-chief for LivingBetter50.com

"*Related by Chance, Family by Choice* came along at the right time for me, because just a few days ago my son married a woman who has captured my heart. I want my new daughter-in-law and my son to have a great relationship, and I want to be a supportive, encouraging mom, but I'm sure there'll be days when we won't see eye-to-eye on things. . . . With godly wisdom, insight, and abundant ideas and tips, Deb DeArmond equips 'women-in-law' who love the same man with all they need to do life together well. The book is an excellent resource that I will refer to again and again."
—**Twila Belk** (aka the Gotta Tell Somebody Gal), Writer, speaker, and author or coauthor of five books, including *I Believe in Healing* and *I Believe in Heaven*

"With candor and a touch of humor, Deb DeArmond shares hard-won wisdom about creating meaningful connection with daughters-in-law and shows how those relationships can be as loving and fulfilling as any family relationship. *Related by Chance, Family by Choice* is a valuable resource for mothers of grown sons—proving that daughters-in-law are God's perfect addition to a family."

—**Cheri Fuller**, Speaker and author of *Mother-Daughter Duet,*
A Busy Woman's Guide to Prayer, and other books

"There wouldn't be so many in-law jokes if more mothers-in-law and daughters-in-law read *Related by Chance, Family by Choice.* Deb DeArmond provides tips, strategies, and stories to assist women in navigating these sometimes murky waters, helping families find clear sailing for the years ahead. Don't miss this book!"

—**Michelle Cox**, Coauthor of *Just 18 Summers*

"I never realized how little I knew or considered about my or my wife's relationship with our daughter-in-law. Deb's in-depth and concise communication gift reveals the necessary ingredients for the family God meant us to experience."

—**Jack King**, Founder of Faithful Men Ministries

"In a world where, more often than not, relationships between mothers-in-law and daughters-in-law are filled with stress and strife, Deb DeArmond shows us that it does not have to be this way. . . .

Whether you are a mother-in-law wanting to improve your relationship with a daughter-in-law or a daughter-in-law longing for a deeper bond with your mother-in-law, I encourage you to read this book and put these tools to work."

—**Gerry Wakeland**, President of CLASSEMINARS, Inc.

"*Related by Chance, Family by Choice* is a terrific tool for *all* relationships, and especially for the sometimes touchy in-law variety. Deb has made what could have been a painful subject into a fascinating relational journey. . . . A challenging book that is also *fun!*"

—**Joann Cole Webster**, Vice president of the
Christian Men's Network, and cochair of
Global Operations for the Billion Soul Network

Related by Chance, Family by Choice

Related by Chance, Family by Choice

Transforming Mother-in-Law & Daughter-in-Law Relationships

Deb DeArmond

Kregel Publications

Dedicated with love to Ron—my husband, best friend, and brainstorm partner. You helped shape this work in ways I never expected. Thanks for being the champion in all I've ever attempted, for introducing me to Christ, and for being the first in my life to ask, "When are you going to write your book?"

Contents

Preface: The Girls

Written on Mother's Day 2011 and posted on Facebook

*M*y sons married incredible women. Each of them followed our advice, and all three "married up." Way up. If I could have selected wives for my boys from a catalog, it would have been these three: Sarah, Heather, and Penny—listed in the order they came into our lives. As we prepare to celebrate Mother's Day tomorrow, I want to take a moment to recognize my girls.

Sarah was the first, and she was also the first one to refer to me as her "mother-in-love." It blesses me each time she says it. I've known Sarah from the time she was thirteen. That's more than half her life, and I can't imagine my life without her. Sassy, smart, and amazing. She is a wonderful mom, and she loves my son Jordan fiercely. She is our redhead.

Our brunette is Heather. I met her when she was sixteen. She is married to my son Cameron. She told me once that when she was single, she couldn't imagine calling anyone but her own mother "Mom." But the bond between us is such that she said she could never call me anything else. What a sweet honor. Caring, smart, and genuine. Awesome wife. She will be an incredible mother—hopefully in the not too distant future.

So that leaves the blonde spot open. And son Bryce filled it when he married our wonderful Penny. "Mama Deb" is her sweet name for me—and I love it. Penny was twenty-eight when she joined the family and completed our set. There was an open place in my heart God created just for her, and my heart recognized her the moment I met her. Amazing wife and mother. Talented writer and runner.

These are the daughters of my heart.

I want to thank their moms for sharing them with me. Dru, Melody, Pam—you all did an amazing job. God bless each of you for the years you invested in bringing them up. My life is richer because I am backup mother to your girls.

And girls—remember how much I love you!

So how did we get here? How have we sidestepped the typical mother-in-law/daughter-in-law agony? What did we do? How do we maintain it? Is it always without its challenges? That's what this book intends to explore. We are *not* smarter, luckier, or more spiritual than the average MIL/DIL. What we *are* is determined to be united as a family and just intelligent enough to know that we can't do it without Jesus!

Acknowledgments

First, and most importantly, thank you to my Lord and Savior Jesus Christ. You rescued and recreated me; You know me and love me anyway. You placed a love of words in me when You formed me and have created the plan, the path, and the push to write this book. I am humbled by Your willingness to entrust its message to me, and You alone deserve any praise that it achieves.

Thank you to my sons, Cameron, Jordan, and Bryce. Nothing prepared me sufficiently to be your mom, and nobody could have loved you more fiercely. I have always been grateful God entrusted each of you to me. I have appreciated your encouragement on this journey, and I thank you for bringing your wonderful wives and children into our family. They are a gift to us all.

Thank you to "my girls," Sarah, Heather, and Penny. Your contributions made this book possible. You each helped me learn to be a mother-in-law by letting me into your world. There's nothing I haven't already said. I love you and am incredibly blessed to call each of you "daughter."

Thank you to Penny Baker DeArmond, my writing DIL. You were a helpful brainstorming partner, generating ideas that found their way to the page. Your willingness to jump in, toddler in tow, to spearhead the conversations with Sarah and Heather, and then capture the voice of "the girls" in chapter 5 was a genuine gift. Can't wait to read your novel!

To the first real writer I ever knew, my big brother, Jack. I admired you so much that writing was my first attempt to get your attention when I was nine years old and you were, well, older. I am grateful for the role you played in helping me find my way to the keyboard. I miss you every day.

To my own mother-in-law, Virginia Rolin. I'm unbelievably blessed by your presence in my life. God knew how much I would need a backup mom. You are my prayer warrior, encourager, and cheerleader. Thank you for raising the man of my dreams.

Thanks to Kathy Carlton Willis—mentor, coach, editor, friend, and guru extraordinaire. I am thankful beyond words (well, almost beyond words) for your skill, your energy, and your belief in my work. Thanks for taking this journey with me. Your friendship is a treasured gift in my life.

To Barbara Scott, my first agent at WordServe Literary Group. You are the bookends in this process. Thank you for making time for me when I missed our conference appointment. Your interest turned into representation and the book contract I dreamed of, due to your relentless pursuit of the right publisher. That you ended up as my Kregel editor seems poetic justice. I am indebted to your commitment.

The sister-friends who encouraged me and cheered me on, who stayed the course and didn't desert me through endless conversations about this book: Cindy Smith, Karen DeArmond-Gardner, Loree Whitsett, Rosemary Graeme, Jayne Gnadt, Eve Clayton, Melody Heal, Jesi Steiber, Pam Baker, Susan Steinbrecher, Diane Bolton, Karen Fox, Kim Rivera-Beattie, and Pat Burke. Joe Malta, I couldn't leave you out. Being the sole guy in the group is not new for you! Thank you for celebrating every success with me. I love each of you!

To my WordServe Literary family: Greg Johnson and Alice Crider and all those in the agency who support and serve authors as we work to serve Him through our writing. Thank you.

Thanks to Steve Barclift, my editor at Kregel, who has guided me through the publishing process. Thanks also to Dennis Hillman, Dave Hill, and the Kregel family for treating me like one of their own.

Thanks to the focus groups and interviewees whose insights, stories, and shared experiences helped us understand the joy, the challenge, and sometimes the pain that the woman-in-law relationship incites. Special thanks to Melynda Bonner, Jesi Steiber, Stacey Bengtsson, Jillian Thomas, Kim Carter, Katie, Vickie, and Sharon. Also to the hundreds of anonymous online survey respondents—we owe you a debt of gratitude.

What's the Problem?

I want to know your secret," said the woman across the table from me. We were attending a three-day retreat for women. I looked up at her and realized she was speaking to me. I didn't know her, and I certainly wasn't sharing any secrets at the dinner gathering. My silence and startled expression prompted her to say more. "I'm sharing a room with your daughters-in-law. They love you. I mean, not just like you. They really love you. I want to know your secret. How did you do that?"

The mother-in-law/daughter-in-law (MIL/DIL) relationship has historically been one of the most challenging many women will ever face. What's the problem? We are two women who love the same man. One as mother, the other as wife. You would expect we might bond over our mutual admiration over the man-in-the-middle. We know the other woman must be bright; she sees him as wonderful too. But that's not usually how it plays out. Each may feel the need to mark her territory as a warning to all trespassers: "Step back! He's mine." MIL has seniority and tenure on her side. DIL . . . well, let's say she may have some other advantages that often trump the mama card.

🕊

The Burning Question

Does it have to be bad?
Can we all just get along?

I've been a mother-in-law for nearly ten years. I have three unique and wonderful women I call daughters-of-my-heart. We know how blessed we are, because our friends, coworkers, and sometimes absolute strangers have reminded us of that fact.

Why is our story so unique? I'm not quite sure. I do know the girls and I have worked diligently to establish and maintain good relationships even when the circumstances and our various personalities have made that challenging at times. We have not always agreed on everything, and I do recall one of the girls asking my son, her hubby-to-be, "Will your parents always have an opinion about our lives?"

"Probably," was my son's reply. "But they won't be upset if we don't follow their advice. They just need to give it." Ouch! His cheekiness in sharing that conversation with us, along with her willingness to discuss it with me, are the hallmarks of our strong relationship. We deal with it—together.

The question from my retreat-mate is not that unusual. I get it often, as do the girls. Many ask us to share how we do life together so well. So as I decided to explore this complex relationship, I asked the girls to come along on the journey. You will hear their voices throughout this book. We often don't see eye-to-eye, but we do agree on some important things: we want to live united, not divided, as a family, and we believe it is possible only if we are willing to acknowledge that we cannot do it without a heavy dose of God's love to guide us.

We have conducted a great deal of research to help us understand the status of the woman-in-law (WIL) relationship. Focus groups, an online survey with more than 150 respondents, and interviews and conversations with more than a hundred women have assisted us in gaining some insight into these unique family relationships. Here is some of what we have learned.

> "The first time I met my mother-in-law to be, I thought she was amazing . . . filled with lots of smiles, happiness. NOPE! She puts on a face, plays a game, and controls the show. Then my husband and I changed the game and she got angry. It's not pretty at all."—DIL, age 34

"She cried when we told her we were engaged. She is very controlling and has a very strong influence on my husband's life."—DIL, age 27

"My daughter-in-law is highly critical of my son and they didn't seem to really be in love when I first met her. I didn't think she was good enough for my son. And I still don't."—MIL, age 49

"I never met anyone so moody as my daughter-in-law. She is desperate and manipulative and tries to control my relationship with my son."—MIL, age 57

These are just a few of the comments from our online survey conducted in November 2011. While many women reported their relationship with their MIL/DIL to be better than average, *less than half* reported it as *good* or *close*. Some facts about our respondents:

- Some 93 percent of those surveyed acknowledged a faith affiliation, and 96 percent of that group self-identified as Christian.
- We discovered that 79 percent said their faith was foundational in their lives and guided their daily actions and decisions.
- In fact, 87 percent reported they were of the same faith as their WIL, but only 38 percent believed the faith of that woman was foundational to her life or was reflected in her decisions and actions.
- Most interestingly, 30 percent reported the relationship was "bad," which they described as not close, difficult, and filled with criticism, or simply off-balance with the woman-in-law.
- More than half (57 percent) said the difficulties in the relationship were either mostly their fault, or they at least equally shared the responsibility for the failure of the relationship.

Given that this audience was primarily made up of Christ-followers, these numbers surprised us. Many women did report a healthy and loving relationship and felt blessed with their MIL or DIL interactions. But the numbers who reported the relationship status as "bad" in our survey were nearly identical to those in a survey conducted on the popular website *iVillage* in October 2010 where there were no statistics on faith.

How can it be that our faith provides us no advantage in this area of our lives? Especially since 79 percent reported their faith was foundational to their daily lives and guided their decisions and actions?

I strongly believe that the routine portrayal of the stereotypical meddling, intrusive mother-in-law who believes "no girl will be good enough for my son" has a lot to do with how we view this relationship. Movies, sitcoms, and late-night comedians all yuck it up at the MIL's expense. Think Marie Barone from the TV show *Everybody Loves Raymond*; Jane Fonda in the movie *Monster-in-Law*; and even comic strip Dagwood's constant, embittered battle with the mother of his wife, Blondie. The MIL stereotype has guided our perspective and our expectations in a subtle but real way.

The Internet is full of resource material, most not intended to help but to let off steam. Consider the following if you will:

- facebook.com/ihatemymotherinlaw—A group of 2,239 women who are happy to share the details of their "hideous hag MILs."
- MotherinLawHell.com—The tagline reads "Daughter-in-law, you are not alone. Stop suffering in silence."
- IHateMyInLaws.com—Orients their readers to the site as a place where "it is fun to hate your in-laws." Daughters-in-law are a primary target here, but no woman is safe; they are all under attack: MILs, DILs, SILs, and even the men, although they get off with a mere smattering of attention.

If the stories are only half true, they are bad. Really bad. One that stood out was the daughter-in-law who now boycotts holidays with her husband's family because the gift she received the prior year was "a hand-me-down, secondhand gift." It was a prized piece of family jewelry, an heirloom highly valued by her mother-in law. She gave the gift as a confirmation of her love for her son's wife.

As believers in Christ, we live in a world that endeavors daily to shape our thinking, our perspectives, and our opinions. It is difficult to avoid the powerful influences we are exposed to on a regular basis. Add to this the real experiences we have observed or the stories we've been told by friends or family who have found hurt, disappointment, or sadness in their MIL/DIL relationships. We may realize our own expectations are low in this regard. We expect little, so when little shows up, we are neither surprised nor alarmed. It is what it is. And we do little or nothing to address it. We've fallen in lockstep with a worldview that does not represent who God asks us to be. We must challenge this lie.

God's Word is intended to serve as our user manual in this life. There is wisdom and instruction on nearly every topic we will encounter in life, including our family relationships. The Bible will guide our path if we will allow it to do so. The stereotypical view of the MIL/DIL relationship is so bleak it creates a perfect opportunity for the Christ-follower to demonstrate the impact of the Lord in our lives by choosing to do it His way and not settle for the world's way.

There is good news. One of the most significant survey results revealed that 70 percent of the respondents said they would be willing to make the effort necessary to improve the relationship if they knew how. That's the focus of our book. Although you will hear our story and the stories of many other women, this is not primarily a book of memoirs. Relationship, like anything else we accomplish, requires not only effort, but also the tools and skills to get the job done. Knowing *what* to do comes from

God's Word. Ideas on *how* to do it are where I believe we can help you.

I have spent nearly thirty years working with adults to improve their communication skills, learn how to deal constructively with conflict, and build better relationships. When my clients are successful, it's not because of the inspiring stories or funny anecdotes I've shared. The successful ones acknowledge that they are struggling in their relationships and are willing to learn tools and skills to improve their lives by changing the way they think and behave in their relationships. They are successful because they choose to be.

Using This Book

To help you get the most from your reading, keep in mind this book's basic structure. Its chapters are arranged to provide a logical path to creating, sustaining, or improving a godly relationship with your in-law:

- The first few chapters offer biblical foundations and God's example for the mother-in-law and daughter-in-law relationship. We will examine the issues that break God's heart and create hurt and division in the family.
- The middle chapters introduce tools, tactics, and tips to move beyond the stereotypical MIL/DIL relationship, equipping you to do it God's way according to the Scriptures.
- The final chapters discuss challenging situations that sometimes create additional hardship in reaching your relationship goals, and include helpful suggestions for resolving the sticking points.

Throughout the book, you may discover some sections that focus on the other woman more than you. I encourage you to read these as thoroughly as those that speak directly to you. Here's the rationale:

Many of us play both roles in our lives. We are both mother-in-law and daughter-in-law at the same time or will be in the future.

Gaining understanding of the issues, challenges, and heartache of the other woman will provide insight for you as you create a relationship that works for you and your family—and pleases God—all at the same time.

In chapter 2, we examine the two most famous biblical in-laws, Ruth and Naomi. Then, beginning in chapter 3 and continuing through the remaining chapters, you will find a brief section entitled "What Would Ruth and Naomi Do?" This section allows us to see how the concepts from each chapter tie back to the lives of these biblical in-laws, their choices, and ultimately, their successful relationship.

We want you to use this book, not just read it! Knowing *what* to do is good, but having some ideas for *how* to put into practice what you learn is even better. At the end of each chapter you will find a resource section to help you do just that.

The format for each of these resource sections is similar although not always identical. In *every* chapter you will find the following:

Self-Assessment. This is a quick assessment to see where you currently stand on the concepts taught in the chapter. Knowing your strengths helps build your confidence, while knowing where you can improve identifies areas for action.

Plan of Action. Here you will have a chance to reflect back on the chapter content, selecting three areas that were most important to you. We encourage you to also record anything you felt the Lord revealed to your heart. Use the self-assessment results, along with your answers to these questions, to create a Plan of Action. The worksheet asks you three questions:

- What will you do?
- How will you do it? (Identify the specific steps.)
- When will you start? (A goal is a dream with a deadline!)

Prayer. The final step in each chapter is a prayer, based on the content of the chapter and incorporating God's Word, that declares your commitment to honoring God in your woman-in-law relationship.

In some of the chapters you will also find Quick Tip sheets. These are kick-off actions or ideas you can incorporate into your Plan of Action and add to your tool belt of resources. These tools will help you make or develop new skills and approaches in your WIL relationship. New skills result in new outcomes. Our goal is that those outcomes honor the God you have chosen to serve.

Life is a choice. God gives us the freedom to choose. But He also makes His will clear to us on this topic. He expects us to choose love. What will you choose?

Take a moment to reflect on your thoughts about your MIL/DIL relationship on the next page.

PLAN OF ACTION
What's the Problem?

Review the statistics and key points from this chapter. Use this information to help guide you as you respond to the questions below.

What were three ideas, concepts, or elements that spoke to your heart in this section?

_____

_____

_____

_____

_____

_____

_____

_____

Complete this sentence: Above all, I would like my relationship with my MIL/DIL to

_____

_____

_____

_____

_____

What areas of your relationship need improvement? Which areas need to better reflect your commitment to the Lord?

_____

_____

_____

_____

_____

_____

_____

Prayer

Father, I recognize that I am responsible for my actions and behaviors in every relationship You have placed in my life, including the one with my in-law. I accept that Your Word is the authority in the life of the believer, and I am committed to honoring Your instructions. I desire to see my relationship with my MIL or DIL reflect Your presence in my life and demonstrate Your glory in a world desperate for You. I am willing to make the effort necessary to accomplish these things. *(Inspired by Psalm 119)*

Chapter 1

What's Love Got to Do with It?

*T*his is my mother-in-love, Deb." The young woman behind the counter in the green apron smiled at me and waved. She was Sarah's Starbucks boss, and I was glad to meet her. I was thrilled, however, with my daughter-in-law's introduction of me. "Mother-in-love" was a sweet surprise, and I was once again reminded why this lovely girl had captured not only my son's heart, but mine as well.

Sarah was the first of the young women who became my daughter through marriage. Our son Jordan met Sarah in the eighth grade when they were thirteen. She was a cute little red-head who melted our hearts quickly. It wasn't long before the two of them were in a full-on junior high school crush.

Jordan and Sarah married at nineteen. While his dad and I would have liked for them to be older, we supported their decision. They were quick to remind us that we, too, had married at nineteen—and look how well that turned out. They had a plan, and when they requested our blessing, we gave it. Sarah had lost her own dad when she was only five. And though her mother would "give her away," Sarah asked Jordan's dad, Ron, to walk her down the aisle. He did so proudly, his eyes filled with tears.

Mother-in-love is what Sarah calls me when she introduces me to friends or coworkers. It touches my heart and makes me smile when she says it. It is a wonderful honor. It also makes me think about the terms *in-law* and *in-love*.

I was intrigued by the contrast of these two titles. Love versus law. The more I meditated on them, the more interested I became. Where did the term *in-law* originate?

The explanation is simple: we are in-laws because of the legal joining of the couple. We are related according to and through the law.

Next on my quest was to understand what the term *law* means. What are its attributes? How does it serve? Who does it protect?

The law has specific qualities and characteristics that distinctly define it.

- The law limits and excludes.
- The law is a finite thing: black and white, inflexible, focused on minute details.
- The law is conditional: if you, then I.
- The law is of the mind and intellect.
- The law seeks to benefit itself. Its only fulfillment is to be obeyed.
- The law is without emotion and without mercy, and it pronounces judgment.
- The law demands a high price to be paid if it is not observed correctly.
- The law is designed to rule by power; it enforces norms and standards of behavior.
- The purpose of the law includes a coercive effect in regulating conduct.

If a personal or family relationship is ruled by law, it leaves a lot to be desired, doesn't it? The law is inflexible and coercive, enforcing standards established through harsh penalty. It is relationship based on the conditional proposition that if you do as I require, then I will not punish you, or I may even provide you with some benefit. Wasn't that the arrangement between God and man after the Fall in the garden and before the death of Christ on our behalf?

Relationship between God and man before grace was built on the Law given to Moses. The book of Leviticus provides a thorough and detailed description of the requirements by which man could maintain relationship with God. There was a lot of blood involved. It required daily attention and a constant investment of time. The next required act of obedience was never far from one's mind, because the penalties for failing to follow the Law were substantial.

Sounds like some in-law relationships I know. Characterized by demand and obedience, inflexibility and personal preference, these relationships choke out the potential for family unity and harmony. Grudges are nursed like babies at the breast. Walls are erected, bridges are burned, and the structure of the family divides like the waters of the Red Sea.

But love is quite another matter. The characteristics of love are very different.

- Love is a living thing.
- Love overlooks, forgives, and grants pardon.
- Love includes and gathers in.
- Love is easily satisfied and does not demand on its own behalf.
- Love is unconditional.
- Love is from the heart and seeks to benefit others at the expense of itself.
- Love is fulfilled when it's invested and given away.
- Love is full of mercy.
- Love pays the price.

Now that's more like it. There's an element of promise, hope, and possibility in a relationship rooted and grounded in love. Look at these—law and love—side by side. The contrast is startling:

The law limits and excludes. The law is of the mind and intellect.	Love includes and gathers in; it is limitless; it is from the heart and seeks to benefit others at expense of self.

The law is black and white, inflexible, focused on minute details.	Love overlooks, forgives, and grants pardon.
The law is conditional: if you, then I.	Love is unconditional.
The law seeks to benefit itself. Its only fulfillment is to be obeyed.	Love is fulfilled when it is given away.
The law is without emotion and without mercy, and it pronounces judgment.	Love is full of mercy and suspends judgment.
The law demands a high price to be paid if it is not observed correctly.	Love pays the price.
The law is designed to rule by power; it enforces norms and standards of behavior.	Love is easily satisfied and does not demand on behalf of self.

The Burning Question

**Should we be living our in-law relationship
in love or under the law?**

It's not a surprise that the Word of God provides us direction.

Owe nothing to anyone—except for your obligation to love one another. If you love your neighbor, you will fulfill the requirements of God's law. (Rom. 13:8)

Let us think of ways to motivate one another to acts of love and good works. (Heb. 10:24)

Jesus Himself gives us great clarity on the topic of loving one another.

> Jesus replied, "'You must love the Lord your God with all your heart, all your soul, and all your mind.' This is the first and greatest commandment. A second is equally important: 'Love your neighbor as yourself.'" (Matt. 22:37–39)

Christ calls the second commandment equally important. To love our neighbor as ourselves is given the same priority as loving God with every bit of our being. And what of the law? What are Christ-followers to understand about the law of Moses?

> I know it is important to love him with all my heart and all my understanding and all my strength, and to love my neighbor as myself. This is more important than to offer all of the burnt offerings and sacrifices required in the law. (Mark 12:33)

Love accomplishes what the law cannot. And love is a choice. Christ chose to love us when we were anything but lovable. He knew every last secret, every shred of pride and rebellion, every ugly thought. All of it. He loved us still. And He asks us to do the same to a lost and dying world.

Demonstrating love on a daily basis is not easy. Some people are hard to love. They are difficult, arrogant, opinionated, prideful, selfish, and the list goes on. It does not matter to Christ. To love those who are lovable is nothing special—those who walk without Jesus can manage that. He asks us to love those whose behavior is hurtful and damaging.

> You have heard that it was said, "You shall love your neighbor and hate your enemy." But I say to you, love your enemies, bless those who curse you, do good to those who hate you, and pray for those who spitefully use you and persecute you, that you may be sons of your Father in heaven; for He makes

His sun rise on the evil and on the good, and sends
rain on the just and on the unjust. For if you love
those who love you, what reward have you? Do not
even the tax collectors do the same? And if you greet
your brethren only, what do you do more than others? Do not even the tax collectors do so? (Matt.
5:43–47 NKJV)

That's a tall order. Being civil is not sufficient. Love those who
seem determined to take you down, to hurt and demean you.
Pray for the ones who use you in a spiteful way. Remember that
before we trusted in Christ, we were just as unlovely in the eyes
of a perfect and spotless Lord Jesus. If we can't or won't make
this our goal, we are failing to follow the foundations of life in
Christ.

Love should define our lives as Christians and should be the
backbone of any relationship and interaction we have. We are
to model our love for one another after the love God has shown
us. Love seeks to benefit others at the expense of itself. The law
demands to be satisfied at the expense of others.

You may be thinking at this point, "Check, please! You
clearly don't know my in-law. You don't know what she's done!"
You are absolutely right, I don't. But God does—and He sent
His Son to die for her. We will explore the really hard cases,
where the level of animosity and anger has created a breakdown
in the relationship. For now, though, in principle, we are asking
that you make a choice. Your relationship approach is a matter
of choice. If you choose to follow the character of Christ and
demonstrate love despite the behavior of the other woman, you
allow God to work through you and in her. You are responsible
for the behavior you demonstrate. Let God handle the results.

One mother-in-law, Suzanne, shared with me how disappointed she was in her relationship with her son's wife, who was
not a believer in Christ. Her DIL, Anna, had made a point of
reminding her, "You are *not* my mother. I don't want your opinions. And don't preach at me." Invitations to lunch were rejected.

Holidays were spent with Anna's family—Suzanne and her husband were not included. The older woman was heartbroken. Her DIL's response reminded her of what she had observed in her own mother's relationship with *her* mother-in-law, Suzanne's grandmother.

"My dad's mother has been gone many years. She died when I was only twelve years old, but I remember how bossy my grandmother was—and so critical of everything my mother did or didn't do. Mom said that although she had tried for the first few years, nothing she did seemed to change the tension between them. She told me she dreaded every visit and was glad Grandma lived five hundred miles away. I was aware of the conflict, even as a kid, and it made me uncomfortable every moment she visited. I was always glad to see her bags near the door, ready to depart."

Suzanne's two older sisters and many of her friends struggled in their own marriages with their MILs as well. Suzanne's husband's mother died when Suzanne had been married less than a year. While the relationship had been cordial, it wasn't particularly close.

Suzanne began to believe that she had been naïve to hope it might be different than what she had observed in her own family. Bitterness toward Anna formed in Suzanne's heart. "My experience with this young woman was very negative. The only time Anna was ever nice to me was when they needed money. The message was clear: your checkbook is always welcome. You, however, are not."

That experience soon translated into a strong belief. "I was convinced Anna had tricked Daniel into marrying her, and I was certain she was not God's choice for him." As a result of her belief, Suzanne's behavior focused on her daughter-in-law. "I stopped trying to get her to like me. I told her that I thought she was lazy and a poor mother. I simply did not care about her feelings. She certainly hadn't cared about mine."

The young wife complained to her husband, and Daniel sided with her when speaking to Anna herself. But when Mom complained to him, Daniel agreed that his wife could be difficult and assured his mother that Anna was to blame. Each woman felt vindicated, championed by the husband/son. But in truth, the man-in-the-middle was just trying to keep the peace and stay out of the drama.

The two women avoided one another and rarely spent any time together. Daniel visited his parents without his wife, but Suzanne felt he was often doing what his parents expected—more of an obligation than a desire to spend time with them. The visits were brief, and as time went on, occurred less and less often.

When Daniel was called to active duty overseas, however, things changed. Suzanne recalled her own early years of marriage, marked by separation from her husband serving far from home. Her attitude toward her daughter-in-law softened a bit. She knew Anna was lonely, isolated, with no car, a small baby, and living a long way from her own family. Suzanne prayed for her daughter-in-law, and the Lord encouraged Suzanne to reach out to Anna. He asked her to extend love to her, to let Him heal the hurts of the past experiences the two had together. The Lord took her to passages of Scripture about loving those who were unlovely.

Suzanne began to call Anna on occasion, checking in, offering to take her daughter-in-law grocery shopping or out to lunch, a luxury not often enjoyed on a military family's salary.

At first, Anna was abrupt and suspicious when the calls came from her mother-in-law. She politely declined. She believed there was an ulterior motive—that Suzanne hoped her daughter-in-law would share news from Daniel overseas. He used the few phone calls he was able to make and his limited moments of Internet availability to communicate with his wife, not his mother. Suzanne responded by dropping her a note of encouragement from time to time and e-mailing her to say hello.

Eventually, more out of need than interest, Anna agreed to let Suzanne give her a lift to the bank followed by lunch together. She was surprised that her time with Suzanne was not terrible, as she had expected to be interrogated for news from Daniel.

They talked about the baby and other topics Anna considered to be safe. As they pulled up to her apartment at afternoon's end, Suzanne asked Anna if they might be able to start over with their relationship. She apologized for the role she had played in making things difficult and uncomfortable between them. She acknowledged she had said things that were hurtful and unkind. And she asked if Anna would forgive her.

Anna was stunned. This was not the Suzanne she had come to know and dislike. This woman seemed different. Better. Anna nodded and slipped out of the car without further discussion.

The change didn't happen overnight, and it wasn't without its setbacks, but the relationship between the two began to change from that day on. It continues to improve and grow as Suzanne reaches out to love Anna as her daughter. She has shared Christ with her, and Anna has been open enough to ask some questions. Does Suzanne still believe her son could have done a better job of picking a wife? Perhaps. But she is clear that Anna *is* his choice, and Suzanne is committed to honoring his choice and doing everything she can to support the marriage.

How did this happen? Suzanne made a choice. She blinked. She made the first move. Their story also helps us to understand how these relationships get fouled up in the first place.

The problems are shaped by our experiences in life—they are imprinted on us, on our hearts and minds. They are real to us. We were there. No one can talk us out of our experiences. Our experiences create in us a set of beliefs. Those beliefs direct the actions we take, and the actions we take in life determine our world or the environment we live in.

Let's look at an example.

> *Experience.* I eat in a local restaurant and end up in the hospital with food poisoning.
> *Belief.* The restaurant has poor sanitation and food handling processes. They don't care about their customers.
> *Action.* I do not return and I encourage others not to patronize the restaurant.

World. That restaurant is off my list and is not part of my dining-out experience ever again.

My action seems to be a rational and logical choice based on my experience. But what about my friend Cindy? She has also been to the restaurant. She loved the food, she did not get ill, and she had a great evening dining out with friends. Here's how her experience plays out:

Experience. Cindy has dinner, loves the food, and has a great evening with friends.

Belief. What a great restaurant! Fresh, high-quality ingredients transformed by a talented chef. The owners care about their customers' experience, evidenced by attention to detail.

Action. She raves about the restaurant and quickly books them to cater an upcoming event in her home.

World. Her party is a big hit, and she is the toast of the town. Many of her friends try the restaurant at her recommendation.

So whose experience is more real? Hers or mine? Which one is more valid? They *both* are—each is valid and absolutely real. But they are different. We come away with very different experiences, which result in opinions at opposite ends of the continuum. Here's where it gets interesting.

Cindy invites me to the gathering in her home. I am impressed by the presentation of the food and absolutely love the unique flavors and combinations of each dish served. I speak with my husband several days later, and we decide to engage the same caterer for his mother's seventy-fifth birthday party which we are planning. When I phone Cindy to get the name and contact information of the caterer, I am shocked to discover it's the same restaurant that landed me in the hospital only a month ago.

I have had two different experiences with the same restaurant. Those two different experiences produced two different sets of beliefs. My original opinion is now challenged—not by someone else's recommendation or experience, but by my own second, positive experience. I am now forced to reconsider my first belief. It's possible the restaurant was having a bad night. They might have received food from a supplier that was not fresh. Maybe it was the pushcart hot dog I had earlier in the day that was the culprit. Or maybe I never pinpoint exactly where the problem began. But I am now willing to reconsider my original perspective and take a different course of action as a result.

How does this apply to Suzanne and Anna?

Experience. Suzanne had seen her mother's bad experience with her grandmother. The same pattern was repeated in the marriages of her sisters and many friends. She had not seen many good examples of the MIL/DIL relationship.

Belief. Suzanne believed she had been naïve to expect a good relationship with her DIL, and when her initial experience with Anna was bad, she believed Anna had tricked Daniel into marriage and she wasn't good enough for him. She came to accept the belief that relationships between MILs and DILs were simply not ever going to be good.

Action. Suzanne's actions reflected her beliefs. She became bitter and began to criticize her daughter-in-law's parenting skills and told her she was lazy. She stopped trying to build the relationship, nor did she concern herself with Anna's feelings. She complained to Daniel about his wife.

World. As a result, Anna and Suzanne's relationship broke down. They discontinued even the pretense of being family. Daniel's relationship with his parents became strained as well, as he tried to satisfy both of the women in his life. This family's world was impacted significantly as they struggled in the sadness of their choices.

Is there hope for a different/better outcome? Yes! By creating new experiences, we end up with different outcomes. Suzanne made a new choice when she allowed the Lord to soften her heart.

She worked to create new experiences with Anna. Here's how this looks:

Experience. Suzanne allowed Christ to influence her thinking. He reminded her of her own lonely experience as a military wife. Her heart softened, and she began to pray for Anna. She studied the Scriptures about loving others and developed an understanding of one of the greatest commandments: to love one another.

Belief. Suzanne began to understand that much of the relationship trouble had been her own responsibility. She began to believe it important to honor her son's choice in Anna as his wife. Suzanne believed that reuniting the family was possible and that she had an opportunity and responsibility to acknowledge her missteps and help to heal the relationship.

Action. Suzanne took action and reached out to Anna. She didn't let her DIL's early resistance stop her attempts to connect with her. She sent her notes of encouragement and continued to call and invite her to spend time together. She apologized for her earlier approach and asked Anna to forgive her. Anna did so.

World. As a result, Anna and Suzanne's relationship improved. They spent more companionable time together. Suzanne shared Christ with Anna, who seemed interested. It was not without its challen139

ges, but the relationship is on a much more solid footing. Daniel returned home to discover a world different from the one he had left. He and Anna spent last Christmas with Suzanne and her husband. It was a wonderful time for the entire family.

Although this example casts the MIL in the "bad guy" role initially, Anna was prickly in her interactions as well. She had her own concepts of how this relationship should work, based on her own experiences, which we did not even explore. Many

DILs have so little hope for a positive relationship with their husband's mother that they put little or no effort into the relationship at all. It's an equal-opportunity nightmare in the making.

To live with a legalistic view of another person causes a breakdown of the relationship. We cannot perform at the level of the law. We were never meant to. It is why God sent His Son. The law is not meant to establish or maintain personal relationships. Our relationship with Christ is not based on law but on love. He calls us to cultivate the same kind of relationship with others, including our women-in-law.

Love is a choice. Love honors our Father's love for us as well as the sacrifice Jesus made for us. Love heals. Love reunites. Love works. And it will work even in the mother-in-law/daughter-in-law relationship, no matter its current condition. Love never fails.

So let's discover your current condition. Take the assessment on the next page to help establish a baseline for your relationship as it is today. Be honest with yourself as you take this assessment. Remember, you can't change anyone but you.

SELF-ASSESSMENT: LOVE OR LAW?

Circle the numbers that best represent your agreement with each statement. Use the directions below to determine your score.

		Strongly Disagree		Disagree		Somewhat Agree		Strongly Agree
1.	When my in-law and I disagree, issues are often unresolved and can produce tension between us and sometimes even others in the family, but it's better than creating a fuss.	7	6	5	4	3	2	1
2.	I am not surprised that my in-law relationship is challenging or difficult. I think it's typical of the MIL/DIL relationship.	7	6	5	4	3	2	1
3.	My in-law criticizes me, and as a result, I have been critical of her.	7	6	5	4	3	2	1
4.	My in-law brings pain, hurt, or damage into my life and has never asked for forgiveness. I cannot overlook that.	7	6	5	4	3	2	1
5.	As a DIL, my marriage has been negatively impacted by my MIL, or as a MIL, my relationship with my son has been negatively impacted by my DIL.	7	6	5	4	3	2	1
6.	I have spoken negatively about my in-law to others in the family to warn them so they know who she really is.	7	6	5	4	3	2	1
7.	My in-law speaks negatively about me to others in the family, but I don't care.	7	6	5	4	3	2	1
8.	I believe my life would be better if we interacted less often. I limit the time we spend together.	7	6	5	4	3	2	1
9.	We have decreased the amount of time we spend with my in-law to avoid conflict and tension.	7	6	5	4	3	2	1
10.	I do not expect the relationship to improve. It is what it is.	7	6	5	4	3	2	1

YOUR SCORE:
Add all the circled numbers. Write the sum in the box:

70–61 Healthy Relationship   40–21 Opportunities for Growth
60–41 Strong Relationship   20–10 Important to Change Behavior

PLAN OF ACTION
Living in Love, Not the Law!

Review the tips from this chapter, and also your self-assessment score. Use this information to help guide you as you respond to the questions below.

What were the three key points that spoke to your heart in this section? Are there areas in which you've dealt with your WIL according to the law rather than love?

_____

_____

_____

_____

_____

_____

_____

_____

Stop for a moment and ask the Lord to reveal to you any lessons He desires to add to your understanding.

_____

_____

_____

_____

_____

Write out your action plan.
- WHAT will you do?

_____

_____

_____

_____

_____

_____

_____

_____

- HOW will you do it? (Identify the specific steps.)

_____

_____

_____

_____

_____

_____

_____

_____

_____

_____

_____

_____

_____

_____

_____

_____

_____

- WHEN will you start? (A goal is a dream with a deadline!)

_____

_____

_____

Prayer

Father, thank You that You sent Christ to fulfill the Law and set me free to live in You. I desire to follow Your example by walking in Your steps, fulfilling the commandment to walk in love in my relationship with my in-law. I declare in my life that I will choose love, not law, when dealing with her. I hold to the promise of Your Word—and I believe that love never fails. *(Inspired by Rom. 10:4; 1 Peter 2:21; John 13:34)*

Women of the Word: Ruth and Naomi

I expected to marry a man whose mother was a strong Christian who would welcome me with open arms. I believed we'd have a loving, close relationship and be family in every sense of the word."

Lindsay, married less than two years, shared her story with the roomful of women. "I was stunned that my intended's mother was angry and cold at the news of our engagement. Joel had warned me about his mom, but truthfully, I believed I would quickly win her over. I was, after all, Joel's soul mate. His mom *is* a Christian, and he and I were certain God brought us together. I assumed his mother would see it too. I was wrong," she added quietly.

Lindsay's future mother-in-law made it clear from the beginning that she was not interested in Lindsay. "I invited her to help with the wedding planning, hoping she might see how much I loved her son—and how much I wanted a relationship with her." It proved to be unsuccessful. The wedding day itself was tense, as were the next several months. "When I asked to be included in dinner invitations she extended to Joel, her answer was simply no."

Looking back, certain indicators might have predicted life as newlyweds wouldn't be easy for Lindsay and Joel.

Joel's mother had experienced a good deal of sadness in her life. Her brief marriage to Joel's father ended bitterly. A second baby died at birth, leaving Joel an only child. His mother is not close to her own family, and she never remarried. Joel had been her whole life, and in some ways, the head of the house. When Joel chose Lindsay, it felt like one more rejection—abandonment all over again.

There are similarities in Lindsay's story and that of perhaps the most famous in-laws in the Bible—Ruth and Naomi.

- Widowhood left Naomi single and alone.
- Death took not one but both of Naomi's children.
- Moving to Moab meant Naomi was estranged from her home, her family, and her faith.
- Difficulties in life caused Naomi to become bitter.

The story of Naomi and her daughter-in-law, Ruth, gives us insight about what can happen if God is involved in the relationship. In four brief chapters, these two women move from famine to family and a future in the Lord. While you may be familiar with the story, let's explore it with the intent of identifying the steps to a successful outcome—for everyone involved.

Famine sends Naomi, her husband, and their two sons from their home in Bethlehem to Moab. The sons marry Moabite women, but the hardship continues when first Naomi's husband dies, and then both of her sons die as well. Neither of her sons had children, so even the expected gift of grandchildren for a woman late in life is absent. With no food and no family except her two daughters-in-law, Naomi can envision no future ahead. She makes a decision to return to the only place where she knows she might encounter the God of her youth—Bethlehem.

She and her daughters-in-law, Ruth and Orpah, begin to travel together toward Naomi's Israel, where there are rumors of God's favor on the land and its people. But after only a short time on the road, Naomi tells the girls to return to Moab. "Go back. Go home and live with your mothers. And may God treat you as graciously as you treated your deceased husbands and me. May God give each of you a new home and a new husband!' She kissed them and they cried openly" (Ruth 1:8–9 MSG). Naomi blesses them and wishes them well, and they all weep together. This is evidence that even though the women do not share customs, culture, or faith, they have created a relationship that is loving and close.

Both of the young women initially resist, and Naomi offers them rationale as to why returning to their homeland is the better choice for them. The women cry as these truths sink in. Orpah and Naomi embrace and kiss one another before Orpah turns back to Moab. Ruth, however, is not persuaded to leave Naomi.

"But Ruth said, 'Don't force me to leave you; don't make me go home. Where you go, I go; and where you live, I'll live. Your people are my people, your God is my god; where you die, I'll die, and that's where I'll be buried, so help me God—not even death itself is going to come between us!' When Naomi saw that Ruth had her heart set on going with her, she gave in" (Ruth 1:16–18 MSG). This passage gives us our first key to this successful relationship.

Key #1: You Will Always Follow Your Heart

As we began this chapter with Lindsay's story, we learned that her MIL had indeed set her heart toward her son's wife. She, like Ruth, had made a clear determination regarding her in-law relationship. Joel's mother set her heart toward Lindsay: You are not welcome, you are not family, I am not interested in a relationship with you. I will not include you in my relationship with my son. You are not my daughter.

Our words, our thoughts, and our actions will follow our hearts—and they reveal the *condition* of our heart.

Burning Question #1

What have you set your heart on when it comes to your woman-in-law?

Consider the following Scriptures:

> The good man out of the good treasure of his heart brings forth what is good; and the evil man out of the evil treasure brings forth what is evil; for his

mouth speaks from that which fills his heart. (Luke
6:45 NASB)

What comes out of the mouth gets its start in the
heart. (Matt. 15:18 MSG)

Whatever we set our hearts on creates our conversation, our
conduct, and our condition.

This is not merely a mother-in-law issue. It is an equal-
opportunity heart problem. There are just as many DILs who
have set their hearts against the women who raised and nurtured the men they now call husband. "She is nosy and intrusive.
She has no business offering me advice on how to raise my kids.
She hangs onto her son for dear life, but he doesn't belong to
her anymore. I'm not her daughter—she's my husband's mother.
I just wish she'd stay out of our family."

Ruth's heart is also set toward her mother-in-law. Her decision and her declaration reveal her heart:

- I will go where you go, live where you live, lodge where
  you lodge.
- I will leave the gods of my people and worship only
  Jehovah.
- I will embrace your people, your family, your culture,
  and your way of life.
- I will never abandon you or forsake you; I will remain
  with you until death separates us and even then, I will
  be buried where you are buried.

How is it that Ruth spoke with such certainty? In the ten
years or so that Naomi had lived as an alien in Moab, she had
apparently imprinted on Ruth's heart a clear picture of who she
was. Naomi had loved the wives of her sons and appreciated
the kindness Ruth and Orpah extended to their family while
living in Moab. She had worshipped Jehovah God and most

certainly spoke of the true living God with the girls. She lived a life that placed her family as a priority. Even as Naomi urged her daughters-in-law to return to Moab, she did so at her own expense. Naomi was older and weaker than her DILs. Making the journey alone would be a hardship. It would be beneficial for the younger women to accompany her, but she placed their interests above her own.

It is apparent that Naomi's relationship with God had an impact. Ruth's action of turning from the idols of Moab to Jehovah is an excellent illustration of the meaning of genuine biblical repentance. The application is clear: Can your woman-in-law look at your life, as Ruth looked at Naomi's, and say, "I want your God to be my God"?

To summarize this first chapter of Ruth:

- Naomi encourages her young daughters-in-law to return to their mothers and their lives in Moab, placing their interests above her own.
- Ruth pledges her loyalty and commitment to Naomi in every area of her life, from where she will live to where she will die. She accepts Naomi's family, culture, and customs as her own.
- Ruth commits to Jehovah God and leaves the idols of Moab behind.
- Ruth accompanies the older woman on her journey to Bethlehem and assists her along the way.

Key #2: The Relationship Should Be Mutually Beneficial

The second key to this successful relationship continues in chapter 2 of the book of Ruth as Ruth and Naomi determine how they will live together and support themselves in Bethlehem.

The chapter begins with Ruth seeking permission from Naomi to go and glean among the fields of Boaz, a relative of her mother-in-law. Naomi blesses her by saying, "Go, my daughter." There in the fields belonging to Boaz, Ruth catches his attention.

He inquires about her and learns she is "the young Moabite who returned with Naomi." Boaz approaches Ruth to speak with her for the first time in verses 8–12:

> Then Boaz said to Ruth, "Listen carefully, my daughter. Do not go to glean in another field; furthermore, do not go on from this one, but stay here with my maids. Let your eyes be on the field which they reap, and go after them. Indeed, I have commanded the servants not to touch you. When you are thirsty, go to the water jars and drink from what the servants draw." (Ruth 2:8–9 NASB)

Ruth falls before Boaz, bowing to the ground, and asks why she has found favor, why she has been noticed, since she is a foreigner. Boaz replies in verse 11, "All that you have done for your mother-in-law after the death of your husband has been fully reported to me, and how you left your father and your mother and the land of your birth, and came to a people that you did not previously know" (NASB). Ruth's commitment to Naomi and her courage in coming to Bethlehem have won the admiration and favor of Boaz.

She is rewarded for her loyalty to her MIL, and Boaz ensures that she is fed at mealtime. He instructs his overseers to make sure she is allowed to continue to glean and that she is protected from the others in the field. Additionally, he directs some of the grain be pulled from the gathered bundles and left for her to glean.

When she returns to Naomi at day's end, Ruth gives her the grain and the leftover food from her meal. Provision for both of the women is secure.

It is in this second chapter of Ruth that we understand Key #2 to this successful relationship. Naomi and Ruth work together for their mutual benefit. They complete one another, not compete with one another.

Burning Question #2

Are you competing with your WIL, or are the two of you collaborating and completing one another?

Reflect back on Lindsay's story. Her mother-in-law felt threatened by the new woman in Joel's life and rejected by him in his choice to marry. DILs can compete with their MILs as well; for instance, husbands may compare their wives' cooking unfavorably to that of their mothers. In our survey, many DILs expressed that they compete with their MILs in one or more areas. Most often, their husbands believe their moms are superior to their wives in keeping the home. Fifty-one percent of wives surveyed felt their MILs have more influence than they believe is healthy, and their husbands spend too much time with the MILs.

Competition creates conflict and divides. It is a me-first-I'm-tops and occasionally no-holds-barred contest. Law rules the relationship, not love. The goal is to beat the other person and capture the prize—to be first in the man's heart. There is a winner and there is a loser. In truth, there are multiple losers.

Collaboration, in contrast, is accomplished through partnership and a shared goal. There is mutual benefit. There are no losers when we work together. Each person supplies what the other cannot. Just as Naomi had connections and sound counsel to offer, Ruth had youth and strength to work in the field. Neither could win without the other. Together, they both won.

We can learn from their practical, collaborative approach. Thus far in the book of Ruth,

- Naomi blesses Ruth to go work in the fields owned by her MIL's relative.
- Ruth's relationship and kindness to Naomi provides her good reputation and favor with Boaz.

- Naomi is blessed when Ruth provides food for her. Provision is made for both women.

Key #3: Each Woman Should Take an Active Role in Blessing the Other

In the first verse of chapter 3, Naomi begins to think about Ruth's future and her long-term security. "My daughter, it's time that I found a permanent home for you, so that you will be provided for" (Ruth 3:1). Other translations include the idea of helping to secure a husband for Ruth as well as a home. In verses 2–4, Naomi uses her knowledge of the threshing process and instructs Ruth on how to prepare herself to approach Boaz that night as the day's work concludes. She is counseled to lie at his feet once he has fallen asleep. There is no implication of seduction; rather, to lie at his feet suggests submission. When Boaz awakes, Ruth makes her request known and once again finds favor.

> "Who are you?" he asked.
>
> "I am your servant Ruth," she replied. "Spread the corner of your covering over me, for you are my family redeemer."
>
> "The Lord bless you, my daughter!" Boaz exclaimed. "You are showing even more family loyalty now than you did before, for you have not gone after a younger man, whether rich or poor. Now don't worry about a thing, my daughter. I will do what is necessary, for everyone in town knows you are a virtuous woman." (Ruth 3:9–11)

Some commentaries suggest Ruth's request was the method for a woman to propose marriage in this culture. Boaz's reply that she had been loyal in not seeking a younger man seems to echo that possibility. He commits to grant her request, although tradition requires him to submit to the potential claim of another in line before him. He protects Ruth's reputation by sending her home before it is light enough for her to be recognized, and he sends her with a generous measure of grain for Naomi.

Naomi reassures Ruth that Boaz is a man of his word and encourages her to be patient, telling her he will not rest until the matter is settled.

❦

Burning Question #3

Are you blessing your in-law and helping her build a future? Are you investing in her and enriching her life?

Lindsay's mother-in-law made a decision to abstain from a relationship with Lindsay. What long-term outcome can we project for her? If a line was drawn in the sand, forcing Joel to pick, he would choose to honor his wife and any future children. Because of this, he would most certainly decline invitations that did not include them all. The future for Lindsay's MIL was one of loneliness, rejection, and greater sadness.

Although she was heartbroken, Lindsay made a decision as well, taking steps to invest in her MIL and build a future for their family that included Joel's mom. She and Joel began to pray together for his mother. They asked God to bless her. They prayed for God to enrich her life. These prayers produced results, as Lindsay's MIL began to soften in her actions and attitude toward her DIL. "She began by including me when she invited Joel to dinner. Now we get cards from her addressed to both of us—not just Joel. And most importantly, she says, 'I love you both.'" While Lindsay is still hoping for a deeper one-on-one relationship with her MIL, she is grateful for the progress they have made.

In our research, many MILs reported they had tried to bless their daughters-in-law by sharing recipes and tips on childrearing, but were always met with silence or even rude responses. Why? DILs told us in the survey they felt as though they were being judged all the time by their MILs on their cooking, housekeeping, parenting skills—even the way they handled their finances. For instance: "Isn't that an extravagance, going to that grocery store? Everyone knows they have the highest prices in town. All that organic stuff costs twice as much as it should." In our survey, this was the example one DIL provided of her MIL's harsh comments. The daughter-in-law felt criticized for making a commitment to her family's well-being. "We forgo a lot of other extras so we can put really healthy meals on the table. My mother-in-law doesn't see anything wrong with packaged and processed foods. It's what she served when her kids were growing up."

So what the MIL sees as helpful advice comes across as criticism and judgment. The river runs both ways, however. MILs shared that they felt minimized or old in the way they were treated by their DILs when their suggestions were met with, "Nobody does that anymore. Everyone knows that's not how it's done."

It's important to know that any unsolicited advice may not land well. So how can you bless your in-law and avoid this landmine? Here are a few tips:

Pray for your in-law. It worked for Lindsay, and it will work for you. In fact, it's the *only* thing that initially worked for her. Have you ever heard anyone say, "Well, I've done everything else I can think of. I guess the only thing left is to pray." Move it up on your list, girl! And don't say that "Oh, Lord, take her out of my life. Show her how wrong she is" kind of prayer. *Bless her.* Ask God to enrich her life, prosper her, and bless her relationships.

Send a card or an e-mail acknowledging some aspect of who your in-law is—not just what she does. Is creativity her gift? Tell her how much you admire it. Is your in-law a naturally compassionate woman, or does she have a great sense of humor? Let her know how much it blesses you. Is your in-law able to encourage you or others with how she lives her life in Christ or with her knowledge of the Bible? Tell her how it has inspired you—how *she* has inspired you.

Ask her what you can do to support her at home, at work, or with her hobbies, and then follow up on it. After the birth of her first child, my DIL Penny wanted to return to competitive running, but she had made a decision to stay home with their son. Finances were tight enough that the fees to participate in racing events were not in the budget. I asked if she'd like the entry fee to a race as a birthday gift. She was thrilled, and the race provided a goal and time line she used to ready herself.

Heather expressed interest in working in the same profession I had been in for twenty-five years. I arranged for her to observe a few classes I taught, and I used my contacts to allow her to meet others in the industry. She began to network with those opportunities, which helped lead to a new career.

Sarah loves to bake, so I often ask her to provide the baked goods for family gatherings. Baking is not my strength, but I request that she let me work along with her for some extra women-in-law time. We have a great time together, and the family gets great goodies.

Share articles, websites, books, or magazines she would enjoy. The message you are sending here is simple: what interests you is of interest to me, because I am interested in a relationship with you.

Offer help, not advice, when the need is expressed. If your MIL expresses concern about living on a fixed income now that she is retiring, ask if she'd like help in setting up a budget or finding a financial planner. If your DIL is laid off and looking for a new job, ask if she'd like help reworking her resume (if it's an area of your expertise) or volunteer to babysit when she has an interview scheduled.

Most importantly, don't offer unsolicited advice. We've all seen a sitcom in which the MIL knows the only right way to do something, or the DIL bristles at the slightest recommendation. If you would like to share something you believe will be helpful, ask for permission to do so. For example: "I saw a really good article on how to help kids who are struggling with their reading skills. I know you have been concerned about Emma. Would you like me to send it to you?" Asking for permission is respectful and says, "I'd like to help. Would you be open to that?"

Naomi focused on Ruth's best interests and future as her motivation for action. She wasn't trying to control her DIL or demonstrate her vast knowledge and wisdom. Her motives were pure. She used her knowledge to invest in what would ultimately become a great blessing for her DIL. You can follow her lead, whether you are the MIL or DIL.

So let's catch up with a quick look at the highlights of chapter 3:

- Naomi mentors Ruth with Ruth's well-being as her top priority.
- Ruth trusts Naomi's advice and follows her instruction.
- Ruth's behavior, at her MIL's recommendation, once again underscores her good reputation, and Boaz favorably considers her proposal.
- Provision continues for both women in even greater abundance.

Key #4: There Is Always a Return on Love

Chapter 4 is the culmination of the book of Ruth, but it is the beginning of a new life for both women. Let's pick up the story.

Boaz respects the custom of the culture and meets with the man who is first in line to buy Naomi's land. Along with it comes the obligation to marry Ruth and produce an heir, so the land will remain in Naomi's family line. After some discussion, the man declines, and Boaz quickly declares his interest to claim the right to make the purchase and asks those gathered as witnesses to acknowledge the transaction. He and Ruth marry and produce a beautiful son they name Obed.

Naomi declares the Lord's blessing on her life and is redeemed from sadness and bitterness. Obed brings her great joy and restores her to the point that the women in town remark, "Blessed be God! He didn't leave you without family to carry on your life. May this baby grow up to be famous in Israel! He'll make you young again! He'll take care of you in old age. And this daughter-in-law who has brought him into the world and loves you so much, why, she's worth more to you than seven sons!" (Ruth 4:14–15 MSG).

Obed is not just any child. He is of the line of Jesse and an ancestor of the king to come—the Messiah, Jesus.

All of these actions and events were bathed and born of love. From the first chapter to the last, love is active in every phase of the relationship between Naomi and Ruth. And as we know, love never fails.

Burning Question #4

**Are your actions born of love with a pure
motive when it comes to your WIL?
Will you extend God's love to her in all you do?**

You may have a detailed list of all the things that are wrong with her:

- She is not of the same faith.
- She is not a person of faith at all.
- Her culture is different from yours, as are her customs.
- She's of a different race and different background. She's just *different!*

With Ruth and Naomi, all of these factors were present, yet each made a decision as to how they would behave with one another. Once their hearts were set, they followed through, and the Lord blessed them beyond their imaginations.

Love covers a multitude of sins. Love is patient. Love is gentle. Love never fails. Are you willing to walk in the commandments of Christ in this relationship? We do it with strangers as part of outreach ministry. Homeless, imprisoned, addicted—we endeavor to demonstrate God's love to them and accept it as our reasonable service. But many draw the line with their woman-in-law. If blood is thicker than water, are you willing to let the blood of Christ make you family with the woman you may struggle with today?

Lindsay knows from her own experience with Joel's mother that reasoning, pleading, rationalizing, or even offering ultimatums doesn't work. Love did. Love wins. If it seems an impossible task for you to love her ("You don't know what she's done to me!"), then take a look at these Scriptures:

> God, your God, will cut away the thick calluses on your heart and your children's hearts, freeing you to love God, your God, with your whole heart and soul and live, really live. (Deut. 30:6 MSG)

> May the Lord lead your hearts into a full understanding and expression of the love of God and the patient endurance that comes from Christ. (2 Thess. 3:5)

> I'll give you a new heart, put a new spirit in you. I'll remove the stone heart from your body and replace it with a heart that's God-willed, not self-willed. (Ezek. 36:25 MSG)

The Lord knew some people would make it difficult for us to love them. He has once again provided for us in that circumstance. He will lead our hearts into an expression of love. He will replace our hard hearts with ones that seek to fulfill His will, not ours. And He will cut away the thick calluses that have formed and make our hearts pliable once again. He will do it in us and through us. We need only to submit to Him.

Naomi and Ruth are our examples. With all the odds stacked against them, their story has a "happily ever after." There's one waiting for you as well. It may not be easy, but it's possible.

First, you must remember that wife and mother are two distinct and different roles in a man's life. He shouldn't have to choose between them. Both are good. Both are necessary. And both can coexist to provide the man-in-the-middle and everyone else involved a level of completeness, unity, and peace in the family. You might even develop a genuine affection for one another. Stranger things have happened.

In order to do that, we must collaborate and work together to complete the picture and stop competing with one another. Let's find out where you are on that path with a quick self-assessment.

SELF-ASSESSMENT: COMPETING OR COMPLETING?

Circle the numbers that best represent the frequency of your behavior for each statement. Use the directions below to determine your score.

BEHAVIOR FREQUENCY

	BEHAVIORS	Never		Seldom		Occasionally		Frequently
1.	I give advice to my in-law on a regular basis when I think it's appropriate.	7	6	5	4	3	2	1
2.	There have been occasions when I have asked my son/husband to take my side against my woman-in-law.	7	6	5	4	3	2	1
3.	I pray daily for God to bless my in-law.	1	2	3	4	5	6	7
4.	I have issued an ultimatum to my woman-in-law: "If you don't . . . then I will . . ." or, "If you do that one more time, I will . . ."	7	6	5	4	3	2	1
5.	My in-law makes decisions that impact my family and me without consulting us.	7	6	5	4	3	2	1
6.	I use the gifts, talents, and abilities that God has given me to support and enrich my in-law's life.	1	2	3	4	5	6	7
7.	My in-law and I consult one another and plan family gatherings and holidays together; each of us has input.	1	2	3	4	5	6	7
8.	When my in-law and I have differences or difficulties, I pray for God's direction and refrain from discussing it with other family members.	1	2	3	4	5	6	7
9.	I ask for permission before I give counsel, offer advice, or share an opinion with my in-law.	1	2	3	4	5	6	7
10.	Debate with my WIL as to where our family will celebrate holidays has resulted in anger, resentment, or hard feelings.	7	6	5	4	3	2	1

YOUR SCORE: Add all the circled numbers. Write the sum in the box:

70–61 Healthy Relationship   40–21 Opportunities for Growth
60–41 Strong Relationship   20–10 Important to Change Behavior

PLAN OF ACTION
Complete, Don't Compete!

Identify three ideas, concepts, or elements that spoke to your heart in this chapter. Where did you see yourself?

_____

_____

_____

_____

_____

_____

_____

_____

_____

Complete this sentence: I compete or feel competitive with my in-law in the following areas:

_____

_____

_____

_____

_____

Steps I will take to complete and collaborate with my in-law (review the tips in this section):

_____

_____

_____

_____

_____

_____

_____

_____

Prayer

Father, thank You for the example You have given in the story of Ruth and Naomi. The pattern of love and relationship between them is the goal of my heart. I commit myself to pursuing this as a standard, regardless of the response or reaction I may experience from my in-law. I acknowledge that I have competed with her in the form of (fill in the blank) _____ _____.

I ask that You forgive me. I ask that Your Spirit will prompt me to follow through on these decisions. I am committed to the following steps (fill in the blank): _____ _____ _____.

Thank You for Your love and encouragement as I take these steps. I am committed to strengthening my relationship with this important woman You have placed in my life, and am determined to love her as You love me. *(Inspired by John 13:34; 1 John 4:19; Exod. 20:12)*

Chapter 3

Leaving and Cleaving:
What Exactly Does That Mean?

"My mother-in-law is always up in our business," Ashley complained. "She's constantly making comments like, 'Can you really afford that?' or 'Clipping coupons is a really great way to save on your grocery bill.'" Ashley resented what she described as her MIL's nosiness. "She has no right to tell us how to live or how to spend our money. She just needs to butt out."

Ashley is not alone in preferring that her mother-in-law refrain from giving advice. In the interviews and survey conducted as research for this book, it was a common theme. Finances were an issue that was particularly thorny, right along with childrearing.

In Ashley's case, however, there were some underlying issues she didn't immediately volunteer. Ashley and Rob had married while still in college working on their master's degrees. Money was tight, even with scholarships, and it was often difficult to meet their monthly financial commitments. Rob's parents were concerned about the situation and offered to help the couple by sending a check each month. Rob and Ashley were immensely grateful for the help and accepted it immediately.

Here's where the situation gets sticky. Once Rob and Ashley graduated, God blessed them with employment right away. Yet their financial issues continued. Having moved out of student housing, there were additional expenses: a second car for Ashley's commute, utilities (which had previously been included on campus), a professional wardrobe for each, student loans that needed to be repaid, and other items they needed to begin their new lives. They let Rob's parents know they still needed help each month. So the checks continued—for *five years.*

During those five years, the couple established themselves professionally. They also bought not one, but two brand new cars. They took a cruise and enjoyed a vacation to Mexico with friends. And the checks kept rolling in from Ashley's in-laws.

Do you see a problem here?

Genesis 2:24 tells us, "Therefore a man shall leave his father and mother and be joined to his wife, and they shall become one flesh" (NKJV). You will notice this special relationship between a husband and a wife ("one flesh") is unparalleled in Scripture except for our relationship with God Himself.

Although the two had married, Rob had never completely left his parents; he continued to depend on them financially to underwrite his life. A temporary offer of help became an expected monthly annuity, one that supplied the couple with a privileged lifestyle out of sync with the original intent of his parents' generosity.

God is the authority on marriage. Leaving and cleaving is the foundation for family life and intimacy in marriage. It is not optional. It is not a suggestion. It is clear direction from the Lord and is for the benefit of all parties involved.

Because Rob was tethered to his parents financially, his folks felt entitled to comment on the couple's purchases, their lifestyle, and their spending. After all, every investment should produce a return. Perhaps Rob's parents felt their continued involvement in Rob and Ashley's finances allowed them the opportunity to influence them in this area. From their perspective, the suggestions were simply well-meaning advice. Or perhaps the older couple resented that Rob and Ashley were living it up with help from Mom and Dad. Either way, it's a negative outcome for everyone with potential damage to the relationship between the couples.

❦

The Burning Question

So what does it mean to leave and cleave?

Let's take a closer look at leaving and cleaving, beginning with the word *leave*.

In teaching on Genesis 2, Bill Lawrence, a professor at Dallas Theological Seminary for over twenty years, helps to define the term *leave* as it appears in verse 24.

Lawrence asserts that men and women must leave their parents to fulfill one another. Because marriage demands a commitment of the deepest nature, it requires a total identification between husband and wife. "Before this identification can take place, there must be a separation from other relationships which have given identification previously," according to Lawrence. "Because total identification is required for a true marriage, there must be some kind of a separation from any other relationship."[1]

So *leave* is a very strong word indeed. In the Hebrew, it means "to depart from" and even "abandon." Obviously it does not mean we should abandon our parents. It does mean we must change the way we relate to them now compared to how we related to them in the past. We give up our childlike relationship with them, and we no longer depend on them for our financial, spiritual, and emotional strength and stability.

Leaving means we should respect our parents in every way, but not to the point that we allow their thinking to control us. It's an intentional decision of mind and heart. Failing to leave deprives a couple of the intimacy and independence vital to a healthy marriage. Adam Clarke, a Bible scholar from an earlier

---

1. Bill Lawrence, "Marriage, How IT Works (Genesis 2:18–25)," Bible.org, July 7, 2008, https://bible.org/seriespage/marriage-how-it-works-genesis-218-25.

era, in his commentary on the verse says, "There shall be, by the order of God, a more intimate connection formed between the man and woman, than can subsist even between parents and children."[2]

For the moms who gave birth to sons, that's hard to imagine and maybe even harder to swallow.

As vital as leaving might be, cleaving is just as important. What does it really mean?

Returning to Lawrence's exploration of Genesis 2:24: "The concept of *cleave* portrays a vivid picture. It describes glue. When we marry we are stuck *to* (not *with*) one another. For glue to work, there must be pressure applied to the joint where the two elements are joined together." In other words, pressure applied creates a tighter, more secure bond. The pressure throughout history has often been society.

While the pain of the pressure may be intense, it serves a purpose: it helps to cement the bond between husband and wife. We must turn loose of our dependence as parent and child in order to grasp the commitment in the marriage covenant.

We have focused on Ashley's experience so far, but finances is not the only area we must submit to the principal of leaving and cleaving.

There are three ways that a couple must commit to leaving and cleaving in order to achieve the fullness and blessing found in a godly marriage. Those areas of potential dependence are:

- Financial
- Emotional
- Spiritual

Let's take these one at a time and apply what we now understand about leaving and cleaving, beginning with a closer look at finances.

2. Adam Clarke, *The Holy Bible Containing the Old and New Testaments with Commentary and Critical Notes*, vol. 1 (New York: Waugh and Mason, 1833).

Financial Dependence

Seeing our children struggle financially can be difficult. It's tempting to step in to provide some of the things they cannot yet afford. It is important for parents to resist the urge to become the provider. God alone must be their provider. There may be times when He will use a parent to assist, but it should only be as God directs.

Parents have a vital role in supporting sons and daughters-in-law so they can obey this command of leaving to the fullest. According to God's Word, we must cut the apron strings that tie us together in an unnatural way.

Over the years, our three sons have encountered financial challenges as adults and husbands. Jobs that disappeared and car transmissions that blew up without warning are just two examples of times when the money came up short. Some were times when God definitely gave us the green light to help. Those were on an occasional basis, when an emergency presented itself and there was an important reason to assist by lending emergency funds. At other times, His answer clearly was no. Why is that?

In chapter 1 we explored how beliefs are formed through our experiences, and the results of those beliefs are our actions. Our beliefs about spending and saving come from our experiences with money. If every emergency disappears with a simple request to Mommy and Daddy, saving seems like a low priority. The couple can overspend, knowing they have a cushion. Couples often grow closer when they work hard to live within a budget that then allows them to buy the car or house they saved for. It's a joint success. It's accomplishment. And it can bond them in that shared experience as they cleave to one another. It also helps to build agreement about their finances and the confidence that comes with being able to manage their money wisely.

It's important to understand that whether you request help from your in-laws or you offer it as parents, you have entered into a contract with terms that often do not get discussed. When money is owed to the in-laws and a request is made to babysit so the young couple can go to dinner and a concert, it can be difficult for Mom and Dad not to calculate how much that evening out might help to reduce the debt owed. There's not a good way to avoid connecting the two in a parent-in-law's mind, and the topic will often find its way from the mind to the mouth, offending the Ashleys of the world. Both parties must make a decision that the principle of leaving and cleaving applies to finances.

Let's move on to the challenge of failing to leave from an emotional perspective.

Emotional Dependence "I've forgiven Scott. I just wish my mother would. The trouble we had was years ago, but Mom has never forgotten it. I'm tired of her bringing it up every time Scott and I have a fight."

Robin and Scott had been married only briefly when the challenges to their union became apparent. Out of his parents' home and on his own for the first time, Scott struggled with his Christian walk. He began to stop for a Friday night drink with coworkers and spent money he and Robin did not have to spare. The end-of-week socializing became a twice-a-week gathering, sometimes continuing on the weekend. He often came home well after Robin had gone to bed. They argued frequently about both his drinking and the money. Robin felt the man she married had become a stranger.

Upset and unhappy, Robin talked with her mother about her concerns. She felt betrayed and hurt and spent angry hours on the phone describing the changes in her husband's behavior. Robin's mother lived several states away. Due to the time difference, her daughter's calls often came while she was at work. She felt helpless, powerless to fix the problem, and found herself worrying about it nearly all the time. Lacking any other solutions, she encouraged Robin to separate from Scott.

The good news is that Scott "came to himself," as it says in the account of the prodigal son. He first realized he had caused his wife distress, and then he acknowledged he had a problem. He got help, and the couple went to counseling, which provided them with a solid foundation for restored unity. Robin looks back on that time and acknowledges that although it was difficult, she believes they are stronger as a couple because they went through it together. They established themselves in a home church and began to serve in the children's ministry. Seven years later, two adorable babies and the purchase of their first home are just a few of the signs of the couple's healthy marriage and full recovery from their early trouble.

Robin and Scott spent hours in counseling and in conversation at home working through their challenges. Each requested and offered forgiveness. The relationship was fully restored.

But for Robin's mother, none of that happened. The anger, hurt, and disappointment her daughter had described in full detail remained as fresh as when the offense took place. She still didn't trust Scott. Robin's explanations didn't persuade her it was all behind them. Why?

Robin was embarrassed by Scott's partying and overspending. She hid it from their church friends and her coworkers. She didn't want anyone to know they were struggling. She turned to a familiar and understanding person—her mom. Was it wrong for her to have the conversations with her mother? Not wrong, but perhaps unwise. Tearful hours of angry discussion tore at her mother's heart. When the couple experienced reconciliation and healing, mom was not present. She wasn't there to see the joy on her daughter's face or the return of the couple's happiness. She heard about it long distance.

Robin's mom acknowledges that it has been hard to let it go. Mom had spent long days and many nights hearing about Scott's activities—his shortcomings. She lay awake at night, worrying about the couple, fearful for her daughter.

Another factor complicates the forgiveness process: Robin's mother is not a follower of Christ. She struggles to understand how Robin could forgive Scott and move forward with him. She, too, had heartache in her own broken marriage. Robin's experiences brought it all back to the surface for her. It cost her a great deal, and it was a bad outcome for all. The result? Robin still finds herself defending Scott to her mother.

One of the biggest mistakes couples make is to complain about their mates to Mom or Dad. Parents tend to take up for their own children and feel the wounds of relationship as though they personally lived it. Sons can make this terrible mistake just as easily as daughters. Mom can suffer as well. The knowledge that your child is hurting or that the marriage is in turmoil creates a burden. The impact on Robin's mom was both real and negative.

So who is a safe resource when troubles create stress and anxiety in a marriage? Here are some tips:

Go to God. Pray, and unleash your heartbreak on the One who has suffered it all. Ask the Holy Spirit, sent as our comforter, to heal you and your hurt.

Seek out a member of ministry to support you in the situation. Take advantage of counseling services in your church.

Confide in a mature, Spirit-led friend who will pray with you, not commiserate with you.

For many of us, experience in life has established a pattern of running to Mom when we get hurt, frightened, or confused. Part of God's design in leaving and cleaving is for us to alter that behavior. Parents are no longer to be our primary covering. A new covenant is established between husband, wife, and God. Moms need to learn to step back and support that commitment, encouraging children to run to God and one another. Dads need to do the same, but candidly, moms are more likely to get involved if they think their child is being damaged in some way.

We are not saying that couples should not seek support from believing parents. Agreement in prayer is powerful and productive. Over the years, we have asked our married kids to pray *with* and *for* us in some decision-making dilemma or over a concern in a financial setback. They have asked us to do the same. We have come together as adults, not in the parent/child protector role. We do not have to share every juicy detail in order to ask for prayer from loved ones, nor do they need to be apprised of every bit of the story to stand with us in prayer.

Learning to rely on the Lord and your spouse when it comes to emotion is a critical component of successful leaving and cleaving. It provides the potential for healthy relationships between husband and wife as well as health in their relationships with both sets of parents.

The final area we will explore is overdependence on parents for spiritual leadership and covering.

Spiritual Dependence

When we began preparations to celebrate the thirteenth birthday of our oldest son, Cameron, we decided to borrow the concept of the bar mitzvah from the heritage of my Jewish father. The words *bar mitzvah* literally mean "son of the commandment or law." Prior to a child's reaching bar mitzvah at age thirteen, his parents are held responsible for his behavior. But at thirteen, children assume their own responsibility for Jewish ritual law, tradition, and ethics. In other words, this coming-of-age ceremony marks the beginning of spiritual accountability.

As Christ-followers, my husband and I decided this was a twofold opportunity. First, it would acknowledge our family heritage and include our diverse culture in a significant life experience. Second, it would serve to help Cameron recognize his accountability to God for his actions as he moved from being a child to a young man.

There was a third and unexpected outcome from this ritual. His dad and I were also placed on notice that our son was no longer a child but a man in the making. We came to understand the importance of our counsel versus our control. Cameron was learning to make decisions and seek direction for his life. And for the most part, we needed to allow him to do so. We might offer counsel to him, but we encouraged him to take responsibility for as much in his life as was appropriate for a young man his age. We would not allow him to make decisions that could provide a lasting harmful effect or endanger him in any way. But choices were left, for the most part, to him.

It was not an easy transition for us. There were times we failed in fulfilling the commitment we made to step back. But during this time, we became fully aware that good decision making, moral choices, and living in a way that honors God are personal decisions and cannot be mandated by the power of parental demand. If we expected and hoped Cameron would be skilled in the things of maturity and a consistent walk in his faith, we needed to let him practice while he still lived within the covering and protection of our home.

It paid off. Cameron's life reflects a sincere and consistent commitment to life as a mature follower of Christ. We included some type of recognition of this important transition in the lives of his brothers as well. Jordan and Bryce, too, are young men we are proud of, and each is committed to living a life that reflects their faith in Christ Jesus.

As young men, our sons were instilled with an awareness of their spiritual accountability as part of the growing up process. Their accountability raised our awareness as parents, too, to take more of a backseat and let the Lord direct our sons as He desired. When a couple marries, if that spiritual accountability has not been transferred from parents to son (or daughter), a man may struggle to establish himself as the spiritual head of his family.

A praying mama is a wonderful thing. A mama who is constantly trying to steer her son and his wife in spiritual things *as she sees it* is not so wonderful. Parents were never meant to be the voice of the Lord to their adult children. God sent the Comforter, His Holy Spirit, for that purpose.

I am grateful that my own mother-in-law, Virginia, is a faithful prayer warrior for our family. We ask her to stand with us in prayer on a regular basis. Our sons also count on her for prayer support. She stands *with* us, not *for* us. She adds her prayers to ours, and it is a great comfort to know she is holding us before the Lord. That makes for a loving and healthy spiritual resource.

I married my MIL's only son. She scrutinized me when

we were dating more closely than she did the young men who courted her daughters. Years later, we discussed why she did this. "Ron would have to be responsible to lead a wife and family. That's a very different role than would be required of the girls," she said. "I wanted to be sure he was prepared—and that the woman he married would be willing to support and submit to that leadership." Smart lady, my MIL.

If a woman has an only son, as my MIL did, it can be a barrier to letting go. Just as there is something special about "Daddy's girl," moms and sons also share a unique and special bond. She is the first woman, the only woman, in his life for many years. Relinquishing that position can be tough for a mother. It's doubly difficult if he's an only son *and* an only child. Two young women in our focus groups reported an unusually tight bond between their MILs and their husbands that they attributed to the death of another child—a sibling to their hubbies. Those tragic deaths created fear of losing a child once again, even to marriage.

If the mother is a single mom, she may have come to count on him and even call him the "man of the house." This puts a great deal of pressure and premature responsibility on a boy. While the intent may not be bad, the outcome can produce an unhealthy level of dependence on the son by his mom.

These circumstances are not something we can change. But gaining awareness of them can help us gain understanding and insight into a relationship that seems inappropriately close.

If there is dependence, one that keeps spiritual leadership with Mom or Dad, it's time to make a break!

So, DIL, what if your husband never had a bar mitzvah? It's not too late to establish spiritual accountability. Here are some tips, first for daughters-in-law.

DIL—"Make the Break" Tips

- Meet with your in-laws (and your parents too, if necessary) to ask them to support your decision as a couple to accept spiritual accountability. Explain what that means and how it fulfills God's requirement to leave and cleave as husband and wife.

- Thank your in-laws for the spiritual education and guidance they have provided their son as he grew up in their home (provided that they did indeed furnish such guidance).
- Let them know how much you appreciate their availability to counsel you when needed. Tell them that as God directs, you will reach out to them in those times.
- Ask for them to pray for you daily. Encourage them to ask the Lord to speak His will clearly to you.
- Close the discussion with a time of prayer led by your husband.

Are you engaged to be married? If so, you might make the above suggestions part of the special events leading up to the wedding. Host your future in-laws at a nice restaurant for a night of recognition and acknowledgment for their faithfulness in raising their son in the faith. Share with them your excitement over taking full accountability as a couple for your spiritual lives together, and ask them to stand with you as you take this important step. Perhaps present them with a special card or gift to commemorate the evening. This provides a foundation of open communication regarding your separation from parents, as a couple unified in your faith. This shared experience serves as a basis for a respectful reminder if you or your parents-in-law struggle to maintain the commitment.

For the mamas out there, you have an important role in this process! The engagement should kick off the celebration of both the wedding and the spiritual leadership your son will be providing to his new bride. If it's long past the engagement, you may have some delayed letting go to do. Your son and his wife are depending on you for support. He may never be able to step into the position God designed for him without your assistance and blessing. So here are a few tips to help you do just that.

MIL — "Help Them Go" Tips

- Pledge your support to this couple's mature decision to accept God's Word and His plan. Share your pledge with the young couple and someone you can count on as an accountability partner. This should be someone whom you will allow to gently remind you of your commitment should you get off track.
- Celebrate and congratulate your son's maturity. Let him know how proud you are of him for accepting the responsibility of spiritual leadership.
- Pray for your son and DIL daily. Ask God to strengthen them and provide direction. Ask the Lord to help them hear Him clearly.
- When they come to you for advice or direction, resist the urge to provide it immediately. It feels great when our adult children seek us out for insight or answers; it reinforces their need for us. But they need Him more. Ask them first if they have prayed and sought God's will. Send them in His direction and let them know you will agree with them in prayer to hear God's voice.
- When you feel impressed to intervene in their lives, ask God if He has an appropriate role for you in their situation. If so, go. If not, stop.
- Remind yourself that a godly son and DIL are a wonderful gift. If he is a man seeking to submit to God and take the role of spiritual leader in his family—congratulations. You did a great job, Mom!

Leaving and cleaving are not difficult principles to understand, but they can be real doozies to implement for all parties involved. So let's see how you are doing when it comes to living the leaving and clinging to cleaving. You will find the assessment for this chapter on the next two pages. There are two versions, one for DILs and one for MILs.

SELF-ASSESSMENT: DIL—Make the Break!

Circle the numbers that best represent the frequency of your behavior for each statement. Use the directions below to determine your score.

BEHAVIOR FREQUENCY

BEHAVIORS	Never		Seldom		Occasionally		Frequently
1. We are dependent on my in-laws for financial assistance.	7	6	5	4	3	2	1
2. We have requested or accepted financial assistance from my in-laws for major purchases such as a down payment on a house, purchase of a car, or tuition assistance for school for us or our children.	7	6	5	4	3	2	1
3. My husband has complained about me or my behavior to his mother when he has been upset with me.	7	6	5	4	3	2	1
4. My husband takes a leadership role as spiritual head of our home, initiating/ leading prayer and studying the Bible with me and/or our children.	1	2	3	4	5	6	7
5. I have complained about my husband to my mother and shared at least some details of our problems with her.	7	6	5	4	3	2	1
6. I have Christian friends whom I can count on to pray with me and support me when my husband and I have difficulties.	1	2	3	4	5	6	7
7. My husband spends time in the Word and in prayer on behalf of our family. He seeks to learn more about God's Word through attending a small group or Bible study, and we discuss the Scriptures and their application in our lives.	1	2	3	4	5	6	7
8. My mother-in-law gives us and/or our children gifts that we could not currently afford ourselves.	7	6	5	4	3	2	1
9. My husband and I have an established budget and we are in agreement about how we manage our finances.	1	2	3	4	5	6	7
10. We accepted financial assistance from my MIL (or in-laws) for rent, mortgage, utilities, or essentials and were not expected to pay them back.	7	6	5	4	3	2	1

YOUR SCORE:
Add all the circled numbers. Write the sum in the box:

70–61 Healthy Relationship   40–21 Opportunities for Growth
60–41 Strong Relationship   20–10 Important to Change Behavior

SELF-ASSESSMENT: MIL—Help Them Go!

Circle the numbers that best represent the frequency of your behavior for each statement. Use the directions below to determine your score.

BEHAVIORS	Never		Seldom		Occasionally		Frequently
1. My son and his family are dependent on us financially.	7	6	5	4	3	2	1
2. My son and DIL have requested or accepted financial assistance from me (or my spouse and me) for major purchases such as a down payment on a house, purchase of a car, or tuition assistance for school for them or their children.	7	6	5	4	3	2	1
3. Although I do not give advice, I am willing to listen to my DIL's frustration with my son and/or their marriage.	7	6	5	4	3	2	1
4. As the more mature Christian, I offer spiritual guidance and insight to my son and DIL.	7	6	5	4	3	2	1
5. I (or my spouse and I) have cosigned a loan for my son and DIL.	7	6	5	4	3	2	1
6. When my son complains to me about his wife, I offer a listening ear and try to provide him with counsel.	7	6	5	4	3	2	1
7. I do not provide my son and DIL with financial assistance; I believe they need to manage on their own.	1	2	3	4	5	6	7
8. I enjoy giving my son, DIL, and their children gifts they could not currently afford themselves.	7	6	5	4	3	2	1
9. When I see my son and/or DIL make what I consider spiritual missteps, I feel it important to offer them my perspective.	7	6	5	4	3	2	1
10. I (or my spouse and I) have assisted financially with rent, utilities, or essentials and have not expected them to pay us back.	7	6	5	4	3	2	1

BEHAVIOR FREQUENCY

YOUR SCORE:
Add all the circled numbers. Write the sum in the box:

70–61 Healthy Relationship   40–21 Opportunities for Growth
60–41 Strong Relationship   20–10 Important to Change Behavior

PLAN OF ACTION
Leaving and Cleaving!

Review the tips from this chapter, as well as your self-assessment score. Use this information to help guide you as you respond to the questions below.

What were the three key points that spoke to your heart in this section? DIL: Have you left your family to cleave to your husband? MIL: Have you fully released your son to cleave to his wife?

_____

_____

_____

_____

_____

_____

_____

_____

_____

_____

Stop for a moment and ask the Lord to reveal to you any lessons He desires to add to your understanding.

_____

_____

_____

_____

_____

_____

_____

_____

_____

_____

Write out your action plan.

- WHAT will you do?

_____

_____

_____

_____

_____

_____

- HOW will you do it? (Identify the specific steps.)

_____

_____

_____

_____

_____

_____

- WHEN will you start? (A goal is a dream with a deadline!)

_____

_____

_____

What Would Ruth and Naomi Do?

The story of Ruth and Naomi provides a precedent and a clear example for us on the topic of leaving and cleaving. Even after the death of her husband, Ruth demonstrated her loyalty to him when she chose to be loyal to his mother. Naomi instructed Ruth to return to her own homeland, but Ruth begged to be allowed to continue on with her. Leaving behind her own home and religion, Ruth understood the principle of leaving her family and cleaving to her husband—or the only remnant that remained of him: his mother. As the mother-in-law, Naomi understood the concept of letting go of the claim to her son and the rights involved in that relationship when she released her daughters-in-law to return to their own people. But Ruth had already cut the heartstrings to them when she married, evidenced by her heartfelt plea to Naomi to allow her to go forward with her to a new land, new people, and a new faith.

DIL Prayer

Father, I submit to Your plan for our marriage, that each party must leave the parental relationships that have given us identification previously. I recognize that my husband and I must set aside this dependence in order to cleave or bond to one another completely. I commit to fulfilling my role as a wife, and, with my husband, I will establish appropriate, honoring relationships with my in-laws as well as my own parents. My husband and I will discontinue any dependence—financial, emotional, or spiritual—that prevents us from enjoying the authentic and intimate marital relationship You, Lord, desire. If we have tethered ourselves to our parents inappropriately, I repent and ask for Your forgiveness. I thank You for providing leadership and insight to my husband and me as we commit to fulfilling Your plan. *(Inspired by Gen. 2:24; Matt. 19:6)*

MIL Prayer

Father, I submit to and support Your plan of leaving and cleaving for my son and his wife. I recognize that my son must lead his family and that allowing or encouraging him to be dependent on us financially, spiritually, or emotionally is not Your will. If I have made it difficult for him to identify fully with his wife through any of these connections, I repent and ask for Your forgiveness. If I (or my spouse and I) feel led to provide support in the areas of finance, emotional counsel, or spiritual leadership, I will submit the idea to You first and ask for clear direction before proceeding. I pledge to pray for my son and his wife in every area of their lives and their marriage without the need to know specific details. Bless their lives together with happiness that comes from a life fully submitted to You. *(Inspired by Gen. 2:24; Matt. 19:6)*

Chapter 4

Hey Mama! Get a Life of Your Own!

*O*h, you're a boy mama too!" my new young friend said as we chatted at a break in our training session. We spent a few moments exchanging some of the details of our lives as we got to know one another. We discovered we are both Christ-followers, and we were each blessed to have sons.

"I am a mother of boys. How many sons do you have?" I asked her.

"Two," she replied. "A three-year-old and one who just had his first birthday."

I laughed. "That's close to the age of my grandsons. All three of my sons are grown and married, and two have toddlers of their own."

We continued to discuss the joys and challenges of raising boys. Rocks left in pockets that end up clanging against the walls of the washer. Stray Legos your bare feet always seem to find in the dark. So many other special boy things she has yet to experience: Little League, voices that change at puberty, and, of course, the discovery that girls aren't so creepy after all.

"I'm not looking forward to that," she said flatly. "Those two are mama's boys."

I smiled at her. "Mama's boys" is not a positive-sounding term. If someone calls you a mama's boy, it's usually not a compliment. She shared with me that she had never left her children with a babysitter—not even her own mother who lives nearby. When her husband had suggested a weekend away, she refused. "Then how about dinner and a movie?" he asked. "Not without the children," was her decision. The thought of them one day meeting a girl and falling in love felt like a threat to her carefully crafted family plan.

"How did you feel when your sons started to date? Do you like the girls they married?" she asked.

"I love each of them like my very own," I responded. "I am blessed to have these three young women in my life and as part of our family. I call them my daughters-in-love."

This young mom went on to tell me she was from a large family—all girls with just one male cousin. The husbands of all of her sisters and female cousins had joined her family when they married. "I know where those men are on holidays," she said. "They're at my mama's house. They don't really see their own families much at all. My one male cousin—his wife took him away from our family. We only see him once or twice a year, and they live less than twenty miles from us. I don't think she likes us much. It just doesn't seem fair." She went on to say how much that concerned her. "You know that saying, 'A son's a son till he takes a wife, a daughter's a daughter all of her life'? That scares me to death. I'm not going to let some woman take them from me."

I remembered when I had similar feelings. I once decided (when they were in preschool) that my boys were not allowed to date until they were twenty-five. And then only with girls that I picked out! But that's not how it works. They had other plans. And God has other plans too.

From the beginning, our children were sent to us for a specific purpose: "Train up a child in the way he should go, and when he is old he will not depart from it" (Prov. 22:6 NKJV). Parents have clung to this promise for generations. Mothers have prayed it over their wandering or wayward children. And God is faithful to His Word. But there is a second important message here that is often overlooked: we are raising them to *go*. We are preparing them to leave our homes and establish homes of their own. To marry and raise families. To live the pattern established in the garden: "This explains why a man leaves his father and mother and is joined to his wife, and the two are united into one" (Gen. 2:24).

My husband and I prayed for our boys every day of their lives. Those prayers included asking the Lord to preserve and protect the woman He had chosen for each of our sons. To turn her heart toward Him. And we prayed that when they met, each boy would recognize that she was the one. I can testify to the goodness of our heavenly Father as I report that He was faithful to grant our request, not once, not twice, but three times.

Those prayers had an important impact on us as well. Each day, as we held our requests before God, we were reminded that our boys were supposed to go. It reinforced for us that they were intended to leave. Our hearts were prepared for the moment so many moms dread.

As the mother of sons, I had heard the old saying, which (when closely examined) can be translated, "Your daughters will always be close, and your family will joyfully expand. But if you've got boys, brace yourself, Mama. The minute they're married, they're gone. You're done for."

That doesn't really work for me, and I'll bet it has limited appeal for you as well. The truth is, they are supposed to leave—physically, emotionally, and mentally. But that doesn't have to mean they are out of your life; it just means that you have a new role in their lives. Finding that role can be tough. It leaves us with a desperate uncertainty that begs for an answer.

The Burning Question

**So what am I supposed to do now?
Just stop being a mother?**

For many of us, mothering was not just a job. It was a calling, a vocation, our personal mission in life. For some moms, the idea is overwhelming that they are *retired* once their children have grown up and moved out on their own.

When we are raising our boys, we are pretty consumed with the day-to-day demands of life. There's little time to think about and plan for life once they are gone. Then all of a sudden, that day arrives with what seems like little warning. We find ourselves a bit estranged from the son we have invested ourselves in so completely. It's hard not to note that since his love interest has come on the scene, he seems different, maybe even a little distant. It's easy to focus on her as the problem and make her the issue. A little hurt, a little resentment, and soon we begin to fixate on why she's not good enough for our son.

When we feel something of value slipping away, it's human nature to clutch it more tightly. It's understandable. But it's the wrong thing to do. We are reminded in Matthew 19:6, "Since they are no longer two but one, let no one split apart what God has joined together." Those words, dear friend, are written in red, spoken by Christ Himself.

One woman I interviewed said she cried so hard at her son's wedding that she was embarrassed. "They weren't tears of joy," she admitted. "I was in mourning. He's gone. So what do I do now? Just stop being his mother?"

The answer, of course, is no. But the focus of our lives, once our sons have married, is no longer the same. We have to remember that he was always ours to raise but never ours to keep. He has become one with another woman, and if that has happened—then congratulations. You helped fulfill an important directive from the Lord.

Once that happens, however, the reality of creating and walking in a new approach to life is critically important. Without a new set of goals, as well as an appropriate focus and sense of who you are now, a slippery slope lies ahead. We tend to go back to the familiar. And that level of mothering is not only unwanted, it is the very thing that will send your son (and his wife) screaming and in a full sprint in the opposite direction.

Take a look at what daughters-in-law told us about this topic.

Survey Says
- About half—49 percent—of the DILs said they believe their husband spends too much time with his mother.

- Some 34 percent of DILs said their MILs had more influence with their husbands than they thought was healthy.
- "My MIL is jealous of me and/or mad that I took away her son."
- "I took her baby away from her, and she just can't accept it—or me. She hangs on and injects herself into our life constantly. It's ridiculous, and it has turned not only me but also her son away from wanting to be around her."

The passion of mothering is difficult to transition. We've loved them fiercely, and it's difficult to turn that down a notch. But if we don't, we will find ourselves with a passion gone wrong.

Protective, Possessive, Aggressive: Do You Fall into Any of these Categories?

Among the most common complaints from both DILs and MILs is that their in-law counterpart is overly protective of the man-in-the-middle, often possessive of him, and sometimes aggressive in her dealings about him. That can be a dangerous progression.

Being protective is definitely built into the DNA of every good mother. We've dealt with issues such as schoolyard bullies and our child's pain of not being chosen, and as our sons grow up, we get defensive against the girls who break our boys' hearts. These heart-conflicts inspire us to rear up as a mama and circle the wagons around our sons. Like a mother eagle who is ready to swoop down and scoop up her young to protect them from danger, our radar is always up for anything that could damage our dear boys.

I remember facing off with a junior high girl who had broken my son's heart. She had the nerve to stand in my front yard and call him out. The depth of my emotional response surprised me. I wanted to step out on the lawn and give her a piece of my mind. Common sense (and my son) prevailed, and I was polite but direct. Go home; there is nothing to be done here. I was tempted to call her mother and offer a little advice, but I managed to restrain myself, much to the relief of my son!

So how much greater will the emotional response be when hitches arise in the giddy-up of your son's marriage? "Protective" moves to "possessive" at lightning speed, rounds the corner, and hits "aggressive" at full stride. All of a sudden the mama instinct kicks in, and you want to climb in the ring and go six rounds with the girl! You don't even need to partner with your son, thank you very much. I can handle this one myself. How dare you hurt my boy? And I don't even need you to tell me the details; I already know who must be at fault.

Oops! It's not the motive that's the problem. We are wired to protect our young—every species is. But that process has a use-by date, and it expires before the wedding.

Are there some extreme cases of abuse, violence, or neglect when we may rightfully feel protective? Absolutely. But even then, we need to provide appropriate support without emasculating the man we raised.

Mothers-in-law reported in the survey that they were often simply "returning fire." They believed their daughters-in-law had become territorial or possessive first and then eventually became aggressive. Whoever fired the first shot, the Bible says not to return evil for evil. The command to walk in love is not optional.

Managing ourselves in the midst of drama is a challenge. That challenge is made more difficult when we have little else to occupy our time. It's tempting to fixate on the situation and replay it over in our minds. Trust me, the voice you hear in those moments rarely recommends reconciliation or peace. The empty nest can become a place to contemplate the problem and magnify in our minds the issues into which we have no business inserting our opinions, our advice, or ourselves. But because it can be mighty quiet in there, we do entertain the thoughts.

The Impact of the Empty Nest

Some of us moms find it terribly lonely in our empty nest. The activities that once consumed us are completed. Braces are paid for, Little League games have concluded, and piano practice has been silenced. We spent so many years focused on discussions with our husbands about the kids that we've forgotten how to converse about anything else. The awkwardness feels isolating.

Some who balanced dual roles of mothering and a professional life now are less than engaged by the career they pursued. They find it dull and confining. Or perhaps they just long to do something different. Maybe they're even called to some new thing, but it seems like any opportunities have come and gone. "Best to leave that to one of the younger girls." "Short-term mission to help in Haiti? Maybe ten years ago, but now? I don't think so."

We flounder as we try to figure out the answer to the question, "Okay, Lord, so what's my purpose now?"

Being needed by our at-home sons was a heady drug and unbelievably addictive. Our children needed us for survival—a level of need that was both overwhelming and affirming. PTA needed room mothers, Boy Scouts needed a snack lady, and neighbors needed car-pool drivers. And they invited *us*! While we were involved in all of this, it drove us crazy. But it reminded us that we were of value.

We still need that affirmation of our usefulness, and the good news is, there are lots of places in the body of Christ to get that fix! Finally, at this time in our lives, we are available and free to explore our options. They're a lot more interesting than driving the car pool. This is not the time to drag out the knitting and settle in for the winter of our lives.

Adventure has no age limit. There are new friendships to build and relationships to resurrect. It's never too late to serve, explore, mentor, study, create, or minister. During this time of our lives when we can make a genuine difference in the lives of others and fully walk in the wisdom and joy we have collected this far on our journey. It's time to shine. We are relevant. We have value. We are *not* past tense!

New interests, new opportunities, new pursuits—all are part of this transition. Seeking them out can help prevent you from "smothering" your children. A new world awaits you, and it is filled with possibilities.

"To everything there is a season, a time for every purpose under heaven" (Eccl. 3:1 NKJV). Each season of our lives has purpose. But it's a bit of a moving target. As we change, His purpose for our lives changes too! The season of raising our sons has ended, but our relationship with them continues—if we can avoid the danger of invading the lives of our grown children and their families.

Finding Our Way, Figuring It Out

"You know what I love about you?" asked my daughter-in-law Sarah one day as we sat in our favorite coffeehouse. "You don't have an opinion about everything we do." I almost laughed out loud.

"Of course I do," I replied. "I'm just not entitled to give it unless you ask for it or the Lord has instructed me to share it."

She seemed surprised. And that felt good. Those who know me well are aware I always have an opinion. Her surprise was feedback for me that I had done a fairly good job of keeping my opinions to myself more often than not.

Unsolicited advice—unwanted opinions on topics like finances, childrearing, cooking, or housekeeping masked in the guise of "I'm just trying to help"—are a recipe for conflict. To your son's wife, it sends the message that what she is doing is not acceptable—that you are attempting to control her and the home she is making for her family. The need to control never comes from a position of love. It always comes from a position of fear. Let it go.

Instead, set your heart to pray for your daughter-in-law, to encourage her, to learn what is of importance to her. I had never been the least bit interested in the sport of running until Penny joined our family. I'm looking forward to attending a race that marks her return to competitive running after the birth of my grandson. I follow her training progress and am excited to see her regaining her strength and speed. I can't wait to stand at the finish line and cheer her on! It has been fun to share in her success, and I'm so proud of her.

When you begin to appreciate the young woman your son has chosen, the need to point out her shortcomings becomes less tempting. Believe it or not, once you see her for whom God made her to be, you stop seeing so many of those flaws and begin to value her in an entirely new way.

My sweet young friend mentioned at the beginning of this chapter is still in the midst of mama mania and loving every bit of it. As we brought our conversation to a close, I shared with her an important lesson I had learned.

"If you make your sons the center of your world," I told her, "you will be devastated, because you will never be the center of theirs." She looked me full in the face, her eyes brimming with tears.

She nodded, the truth of the words sinking into her heart. "How can I get beyond this? What can I do to make sure I don't become a monster-in-law who ends up alienating not only my future daughters-in-law, but my sons as well?"

Here are the tips I shared with her. I believe they will work for you too.

Accept the Word as the authority on family order. The Lord is clear on this. The covenant we make is with our husbands, not our sons. We are committed to our boys, but the Scripture referenced earlier in Genesis surfaces again in the New Testament. Matthew, Mark, and Ephesians all carry nearly identical passages. It is critical that we acknowledge and submit to this principle. We cannot regard family roles as optional; if it's God's plan, it should be our plan.

Pray for your child's spouse-to-be. When our youngest son announced his intention to marry within just a few months of meeting his sweetheart, friends asked why I wasn't alarmed. The answer was simple: I had been praying for her for twenty-five years. I hadn't known her name or what she looked like, but my heart recognized her the moment I met her. I had no need to assess her qualifications or evaluate her suitability as a potential wife. She did not need to "pass my test." I experienced God's peace and was certain this was the right choice. Nearly two years later, that confidence is confirmed every day. Your prayers for your sons and their future wives when they are still young children also help to prepare your heart for the transition ahead. So whether your son is two or twenty-two, pray. Start now.

Preserve and protect your role as wife. My young friend was placing her marriage in peril by refusing to be a wife as well as a mom. She runs the risk of looking across the breakfast table in twenty years at the man facing her and thinking, "What was your name? I haven't called you anything but Dad in years." Take time together to invest in your life as a couple. Spend time as husband and wife, not just as mom and dad. We took time regularly when our children were still at home to get away as a couple and rekindle our connection. One of the greatest gifts you can give your children is the example of a godly marriage. They will seek to duplicate the marital success they witnessed in your home in their own lives.

Prepare your heart for a new role. You may be the leader of the band right now, but get ready for a new song where you will play second fiddle. The music can be just as sweet. When you are willing to set aside your baton, you are honoring God and walking in obedience. I didn't lose my sons; I gained three wonderful daughters. It's critical to plan emotionally and physically for a life without the daily duty of "momming."

The boys did not necessarily want a girl "just like the girl that married dear old dad." We are four unique women, each with our own set of experiences, preferences, gifts, and opinions. What we share is a love for Jesus and the desire to live life together successfully as a family. I had to learn to think of the differences as a gift. Different is not wrong—it's just different. It's incredible how much easier it was to let go of judgment when I stopped using myself as the measuring stick for success. Let's face it, when we do that, the rest of the world always comes up short! One of the greatest surprises I've experienced as a mom of adult children is how much they can teach me if I am open to learning from them. It has been a great relationship builder, and I know we've all grown closer as a result. I already know these are smart girls—they think my boys are wonderful!

Author Erma Bombeck once said, "When I stand before God at the end of my life, I would hope that I would not have a single bit of talent left, and could say, 'I used everything you gave me.'" That is my heart's desire. Don't tightly clutch the role of being the most important woman in your son's life. Explore your new role and expand it to include your daughter-in-law and your grandchildren. Relate to your son and daughter-in-law on a new level as the adults they are.

Use those talents. You've got lots of living to do. The nest is empty, and that leaves you ready to fly. You're free to pursue the possibilities. But it's a little scary too. Many of the things that defined your life for the last twenty-five years are no longer required. You've completed much of what was placed on your plate. But while you may be done, you're not finished!

Okay Mom, it's time for a little self-assessment to find out whether you've got a life of your own or need to create one.

TIP SHEET
Preparing to Live the Great Life!

Reconnect

- Are there friendships you have neglected as you busied yourself with "momming"? Are there people you've wanted to know better? Set a coffee date or invite a friend to lunch or a spa day. Make a list and set a deadline for reaching out to your friends. Then do it!

- Time for romance can be tough to schedule between carting kids to band practice and Little League games. Initiate a date night weekly if possible, twice monthly at minimum. Go somewhere you don't go with the kids (if they still live at home) and make a general rule to talk about something other than the children. Go to the movies, catch a concert, or just walk through a local public garden. Remember why you married in the first place.

Redirect

- What interests have you set aside in order to fulfill your role as mother? It's time to refocus and learn something new. Take a class at your local junior college, a gardening course at your neighborhood nursery, or a cooking class from the gourmet kitchen store. Develop new skills to enjoy and share with others.

- How long has it been since you took time to deepen your knowledge of Scripture? A Bible study or small group will provide you with both spiritual enrichment and fellowship. Find one in your church or branch out to a community-based group that will help you expand your relationships.

- Moms are accustomed to serving others. Don't stop now that you're an empty-nester. What issues pull at your heart? Mentoring a young woman? Serving food to the homeless? Church opportunities such as nursery or leading a small group? Investing yourself in others can help you develop a sense of purpose and an attitude of gratitude.

Recommit

- Pray daily for your DIL or DIL-to-be.

- Withhold unsolicited advice, helpful hints, and offers to help her learn to cook, clean house, or raise her kids. If you have concerns about any of these issues, refer to the bullet above.

MIL SELF-ASSESSMENT: At This Point in Life

Circle the numbers that best represent the frequency of your behavior for each statement. Use the directions below to determine your score.

BEHAVIOR FREQUENCY

BEHAVIORS	Never		Seldom		Occasionally		Frequently
1. I am actively involved in my community, my church, or other association/group on a regular basis.	1	2	3	4	5	6	7
2. I feel lonely and somewhat uncertain about how to connect with others.	7	6	5	4	3	2	1
3. I have set goals for myself for this time in my life so I may accomplish specific things: financial, personal, spiritual.	1	2	3	4	5	6	7
4. I find that I am tired and don't always feel like making the effort to go out or attend functions.	7	6	5	4	3	2	1
5. With my children grown and on their own, I am unsure what my purpose should be.	7	6	5	4	3	2	1
6. I volunteer in some capacity: at church, as a mentor, in my community.	1	2	3	4	5	6	7
7. I feel my kids have more important things to do and wish they would make more time for me in their lives.	7	6	5	4	3	2	1
8. I have a warm group of friends with whom I enjoy time socializing on a regular basis.	1	2	3	4	5	6	7
9. I continue in the workforce and find it satisfying for the most part.	1	2	3	4	5	6	7
10. I am involved in some type of learning activity: book club, Bible study, craft or hobby, dance class, or similar.	1	2	3	4	5	6	7

YOUR SCORE:
Add all the circled numbers. Write the sum in the box:

70–61 Healthy Relationship   40–21 Opportunities for Growth
60–41 Strong Relationship   20–10 Important to Change Behavior

PLAN OF ACTION
Mother-In-Law: Living a Great Life Now!

Review the tips from this chapter, as well as your self-assessment score. Use this information to help guide you as you respond to the questions below.

What were the three key points that spoke to your heart in this section?

_____

_____

_____

_____

_____

_____

_____

_____

Stop for a moment and ask the Lord to reveal to you any lessons He desires to add to your understanding

_____

_____

_____

_____

_____

_____

Write out your action plan.
- WHAT will you do?

_____

_____

_____

_____

_____

_____

_____

- HOW will you do it? (Identify the specific steps.)

_____

_____

_____

_____

_____

_____

- WHEN will you start? (A goal is a dream with a deadline!)

_____

_____

_____

What Would Ruth and Naomi Do?

In this chapter we see both positive and negative examples of moving on with life after change through the examples of Ruth and Naomi. When their husbands died, the women made very different choices. Ruth dug deep into her heart to find the determination required to do the right thing and to make a new life. Naomi, on the other hand, grew bitter. But even in her bitterness she had wisdom to plan for provision by advising Ruth to go to Boaz. When a mother-in-law releases her son to marriage, it's time to move forward and begin a new stage in life. She can grow bitter or she can make a new life for herself. When our choices reflect a desire to honor God and His Word, we can be assured of His blessings on our lives, as we see with Ruth and Naomi.

Prayer

Father, thank You that You have given me life in Your Son. I want to walk in every bit of the fullness of life You sent Christ to secure for me when He died at Calvary. I desire to move into this next phase of my life with clarity concerning the gifts You've given me and the path You've selected for me. Help me see opportunities to invest the talent You've entrusted to me and give it away daily. Show me how to focus less on making my son and his family the center of my world. As I align myself with them as *one*, they will grow stronger as a couple and invite me into their lives in an appropriate manner. *(Inspired by John 10:10; Eph. 3:19)*

Chapter 5

Daughter Dearest:
Be Careful What You Sow!

*It wouldn't be fair or credible for the MIL alone to address
the daughters-in-law, so in this chapter, you will hear from
all of the girls, with Penny voicing insights and tips that
she, Sarah, and Heather created. Though some of the
stories come from our research, most belong to them.*

The stereotypical MIL/DIL relationship is often difficult. DILs frequently expect MILs to be intrusive, highly opinionated, and overly attached to their sons—and often, the DILs are absolutely right.

When Mama Deb approached us with the idea of collaborating on this book, Sarah, Heather, and I were excited to jump in because of the obvious need to help MILs and DILs improve these important family connections. All three of us have examples among our friends or families of strained relationships that create stress in every encounter.

The Burning Question

**I have a mom.
Why make room for another?**

While our relationships are not perfect all the time, we've discovered what works for us. By sharing our insights and experiences along with helpful Scriptures, we hope to help you too find an authentic and loving relationship with your mother-in-law.

During our research, we heard from many DILs in unhappy situations. Some were living the reality of a difficult MIL. Other DILs were creating drama that made the relationship unhealthy. This story from a DIL named Cassie stood out for us.

"From the day I met Jeff's family, I felt accepted. My mother-in-law to be, Sandra, was so excited to have a girl in the family, since she had raised two sons. Sandra told everyone how well I fit in," said Cassie. "It seemed nice."

Jeff and Cassie had met during their final year in college. Jeff was a commuting student, living nearby. Cassie was three thousand miles from her Seattle home, but she loved the university and the rich history of the Boston area. "Jeff assumed we'd live on the East Coast when we married, and in all fairness, we never discussed living anywhere else."

The wedding was held in Cassie's home church in Seattle, and a second reception was held on their return to Boston. Both families agreed the couple made a great match.

Not long after their return home, Cassie had second thoughts about living so far from family and struggled to feel at home on the East Coast. "I was so unhappy. I hated the cold weather, my job was not at all engaging, and I was tired of the East Coast snobbery." Bottom line: Cassie missed her family and wanted to move back to Seattle. Jeff was stunned. Everyone was.

Jeff let Cassie know he felt he could not leave his new job, having been there such a short time. He assured her they would visit Seattle often and suggested that her parents could visit them in Boston. It didn't change her mind, and the situation escalated. "Jeff's mom tried to jolly me out of it and told me it might take a while to get used to living in Beantown," Cassie recalls. "I know she was trying to help, but it was so irritating.

"Eventually, I realized Jeff's family was the real problem. If not for them—especially his mom—he'd be open to the move. They were what held him back."

Cassie avoided spending time with Jeff's folks. "I made excuses for not getting together, and when we did see one another, it was tense." She admits that when they were together, she tried to limit her interaction during conversations, often keeping to herself. "When they tried to draw me into conversation, I was polite but not particularly interested. My mother-in-law, Sandra, just couldn't leave it alone; she would not give up. Unrelenting, she spoke privately to Jeff about it, and he told me he was embarrassed by my behavior."

Cassie overheard Sandra talking with Jeff one afternoon. "Sandra said I wanted Jeff all for myself," Cassie recalled. "That's just not true. I did call him a mama's boy once, but I don't really think that's accurate. But I did feel I was competing with his family. Without them, I'm sure I could convince him to move to Seattle."

Cassie reports that they see little of her in-laws unless it can't be avoided. "We see them at the holidays, and Jeff stops by on occasion on his way home from work. Sandra once asked why I don't like her, and she says they're heartbroken." Cassie paused for a moment. "It's not even about them. They're nice people. They've tried very hard to make me feel like family, but they're not *my* family."

When Cassie vacations in Seattle, she returns to Boston feeling worse than when she left. Jeff recently said, "You'd think you'd be grateful for having the time with your folks." But his words only underscore Cassie's tormented reality: *You are not my family, and I don't want to live here.*

It's difficult to understand what Cassie's expectations were about marriage, in-laws, and setting up a home so far away from her family. Perhaps college seemed like just a temporary relocation. She may not have anticipated how much time she and Jeff would spend with his family. One thing seems certain: she hadn't fully explored her feelings and hadn't discussed them sufficiently with Jeff.

Where do we get our expectations about how our relationships with our MILs will work?

- They may come from our own observations prior to marriage.

- Perhaps we were influenced by the MIL/DIL relationships of sisters or close friends.
- It's possible our hubby-to-be added his own spin on what to expect from his mama.
- Or maybe late-night TV comedians and the stereotypical Marie Barone of *Everybody Loves Raymond* have helped shape our expectations.

Mothers-in-law need a better public relations program; there's a lot of bad press out there. Some of it may be earned, but much, if not most, is wildly exaggerated. Have you believed that bad MIL/DIL relationships are the norm? Have you joined the ranks of those with high anxiety and low expectations regarding this important family connection? If so, you are living with a lie that suggests that the worst is the standard and nothing more is possible.

No matter where they came from, expectations can be problematic. If you thought she'd be wonderful and she's not, you're surprised, hurt, or angry. Maybe you never gave the relationship with your husband's mother a thought at all before you married and now find yourself in a daily soap opera. Or maybe you expected the worst and it never materialized.

Mama Deb's youngest son and I had been dating only a short time when we realized we had a serious relationship. Bryce wanted me to get to know his folks, so we met for lunch and shared with them where we thought this was headed. I was concerned they might have strong feelings about the fact that we had not been dating long, that I had been married before and was older than Bryce. Before we could bring it up, his parents assured us these things were not issues for them. It was a relief to know how they felt, and it set the tone for what I might expect. It also began to shape my expectations for what the relationship between Bryce and me would be.

Some of our expectations are based on our personal experiences with our MIL. One young wife we spoke to, Anita, struggles with her MIL's critical nature and bad attitude. "Most often it's not being her daughter-in-law that's difficult. It's hearing the constant barrage of her negative conversation, always putting people down and comparing herself to others. My husband supports me, but his attempts to discuss it with her have been dismissed," Anita explains. "I love her, but I'm to the point that I no longer want to be around her. They live close by, and it's difficult to avoid them. They expect us to be very present in their lives. I'm just not sure I can do it anymore."

It's important to understand the role God has given the mother-in-law in your life, and what *He* expects. She is your husband's mother and deserves to be honored. You may not like her, but respectful behavior is not optional according to the Word of God. Her behavior may make it difficult to have respect for her. It's vital to remind yourself that you choose your behavior daily, and behaving respectfully is always the minimum standard of care.

What's the outcome of disrespectful behavior toward your MIL?

- You fail to honor God's Word. Christlikeness is nowhere to be found. They will know we are Christians by our love (see John 13:35). Scripture commands us to reach out to those who are harsh; they're unhappy people, often suffering (see Eph. 4:31–32).
- The opportunity to influence her for the Lord has been eliminated.
- Your husband may be terribly hurt. Even if he doesn't love her behavior, he loves her.
- You set an example for your children which, should they imitate it, will cause them to lose respect for motherhood in general and may cause them difficulties in their own in-law relationships down the line.

So what about Anita and her negative MIL? Is she simply stuck with the situation, or are there steps she can take to improve it? Her MIL is a Christian struggling in her own walk with the Lord. She needs support, prayer, and willingness from those who love her to help her move beyond the negativity that has become her pattern. Anita has options. Here are a few for her to consider:

- She could talk with her MIL directly, assuring her that she is loved while expressing concern about her negative conversation and its impact on Anita and her children. Anita could speak the truth in love, using the tools from chapter 7.
- She and her family could move to another state.
- She could create excuses and skip family gatherings.

Which path is the right one? It's hard to know which one will create the outcome Anita is looking for, but we'd suggest she start with the first one on the list. The right road is not usually the easy road, but it's navigable if you have the right tools.

Mama Deb made it a point to create open communication in our relationship from the very beginning by telling me it was a safe place for discussions. If having an open circuit of communication between you and your MIL has never been addressed, be the one to approach it. Knowing that option is available puts me at ease for any tough conversations we might need to have in the future. Words can attach themselves to us and onto others, so be mindful of the words that flow from your mouth. It is important to know how you and your MIL choose to communicate and equally important to think about *what* you are saying. "Death and life are in the power of the tongue" (Prov. 18:21 NASB).

Don't allow fear to take over or keep you from addressing what needs attention. God has equipped you with all you need to approach a difficult conversation. James 1:27 warns us to observe the power words can hold. A word out of your mouth may seem of no account, but it has the power to accomplish nearly anything—or destroy it (see James 3:5 MSG). Approach tough conversations with your MIL with these Scriptures at heart.

If you are already married, the following suggestions from Sarah, Heather, and me can help build your relationship with your mother-in-law regardless of where it currently stands.

Making a Place for His Mom: Tips from Sarah, Heather, and Penny

Build a relationship with your MIL. Explore areas you can enjoy together. If she is showing an interest in you or your interests, nurture that. She's attempting to build a relationship with you apart from being your husband's mom.

Learn how to have conversations with your MIL without your husband as the go-between, unless it's something you both need to say together. Asking him to be your mediator can make the situation more difficult, and it puts him in a bad position.

Learn what your MIL's love language is. Does she respond more to acts of service than gifts? If so, offer to help clean up after a holiday meal instead of bringing her flowers. Does she appreciate words of affirmation? Acknowledge what a good cook (or mom or friend) she is. Knowing what's most important to her can help create harmony. It will assist in communication and help establish a loving relationship.

Remember, this is a relationship for life. Approach it as a long-term investment. Keep things in perspective, and don't let small things become big things.

Be flexible. Once you are married and understand how your husband's family operates, you may be tempted to compare it to your family's methods or feel yourself becoming competitive. Stop before it causes damage and hurt feelings.

Be mindful of the things you discuss with your MIL regarding what goes on between you and your husband. If it's not her business, don't make it her business—that's asking for trouble. She will feel the need to take sides. Plus, she will remember the issue long past when you and your husband have resolved it and moved on.

Once you start your family, have a conversation with your MIL about expectations. What type of childrearing advice, if any, do you welcome? Do you expect her to follow your rules when she babysits? Being clear on such matters is important; it gets you all on the same page.

Let your MIL know that you are interested in creating a unified family and would value the opportunity to be part of discussions that impact the entire group. Ask for shared decision making concerning holiday plans, birthday celebrations, and other family activities. It's hard to feel part of something when you have no ownership.

Remind yourself that she is the woman who raised the man you love, even if your MIL is not a person you enjoy spending time with. Maintain the big picture: you'll be a mother-in-law one day too. If you sow grace and patience now, it will be returned to you. Sow contempt and unforgiveness, and you may discover that they make for a bitter harvest.

Pray for her. Ask God to show you how to love and respect your husband's mom. It's often the furthest thing from your thoughts, but God can do what you cannot: change her heart and mind—and perhaps yours too.

Not Married Yet? Things to Keep in Mind

Do your recon—and do it early in your relationship. You are joining a program already in progress. She is his mother, and that will never change. Take time to learn about her, and the rest of the family too. When you're in love, it's easy to believe that together you can overcome anything. Sadly, that's not always true. One woman noted in the survey, "If I'd have met his family before we married, I'd have been the runaway bride." She discovered alcoholism and a history of abuse as well as mental illness. "I'm not saying my husband has issues with those things, but dealing with his family is a nightmare *because* of those things. I love him, but I'm not sure I'd do it all over again."

Remember when you marry the guy, you marry the family. You may not believe that has to be the case, because "he knows they're crazy and has already distanced himself from them." Good luck with that. When those babies start showing up, so will his folks. Be clear: Are these people with whom you can share your life?

Learn about family traditions, holiday observances, and spiritual values so you are not surprised when issues and differences surface.

Pray. Pray for direction and guidance. Pray for your future MIL. Be open to hearing from the Lord on how to manage your relationship with your future MIL.

Most importantly, have a heart. One day you will understand how it feels to be replaced as the most important person in your child's life. For some moms, it's more painful than they ever imagined. For others, it is viewed as natural and godly. They choose to see it as the family expanding, not shrinking. For all moms, it's a major life change.

Wherever you find yourself on this journey, there are alternate roads to take. If the one you're on isn't working for you, perhaps it's time to reassess your route. Remember, Ruth had her heart set on traveling the road with her MIL, Naomi, to a new place. What have you set your heart on? The best way to get where you're going is to know where you are. Take the self-assessment on the next page to get your bearings. Then use the final pages in this chapter to determine the route to a new place—a better place—for you and the first woman to love your husband.

SELF-ASSESSMENT: Making a Place for His Mom

Circle the numbers that best represent your agreement with each statement. Use the directions below to determine your score.

	Strongly Disagree		Disagree		Somewhat Agree		Strongly Agree
1. I have discontinued my relationship with my MIL.	7	6	5	4	3	2	1
2. I communicate with my MIL at least monthly by phone, mail, or e-mail.	1	2	3	4	5	6	7
3. It's not my role to help strengthen ties to my husband's family. He can do it if he thinks it's important.	7	6	5	4	3	2	1
4. Even though my relationship with my MIL is not good, I think that's normal and I'm okay with it.	7	6	5	4	3	2	1
5. I would prefer not to spend any time, including holidays, with my MIL.	7	6	5	4	3	2	1
6. I pray for my MIL.	1	2	3	4	5	6	7
7. My husband no longer expects me to accompany him when he visits his mom, so he goes alone.	7	6	5	4	3	2	1
8. I enjoy my MIL's company, and we do things together when we have a chance.	1	2	3	4	5	6	7
9. I am willing to take steps to improve our relationship even if my MIL gives me little encouragement to do so.	1	2	3	4	5	6	7
10. When I have a problem with my husband's mother, I think he should be the one to deal with it.	7	6	5	4	3	2	1

YOUR SCORE:
Add all the circled numbers. Write the sum in the box:

    70–61 Healthy Relationship   40–21 Opportunities for Growth
    60–41 Strong Relationship   20–10 Important to Change Behavior

PLAN OF ACTION
Making a Place for His Mom

Review the tips from this chapter as well as your self-assessment score. Use this information to help guide you as you respond to the questions below.

As you prepare to create this plan of action, we encourage you to look at three areas: What is believable, what is manageable, and what is controllable? For example, if you don't believe the relationship will ever be close, can you *believe* for a brief holiday spent together without upset or drama? If you can't see yourself communicating with your mother-in-law weekly, can you manage it monthly? You cannot control her behavior, but you can choose to control yours. What lies within your control that can improve the relationship?

- I can believe and will work to achieve

_____

_____

_____

_____

_____

- I can manage and will commit to

_____

_____

_____

_____

_____

- I will choose to control

_____

_____

_____

_____

_____

Stop for a moment and ask the Lord to reveal any lessons He desires to add to your understanding.

_____

_____

_____

_____

_____

_____

_____

_____

_____

_____

_____

_____

_____

_____

What Would Ruth and Naomi Do?

This chapter emphasizes how essential it is for the DIL to make a place for hubby's mom in her life. Ruth was grateful for Naomi and went out of her way to demonstrate her gratitude by making a special place for her. She gave Naomi preferential treatment ahead of her own needs and honored her MIL even when she was not easy to live with.

Prayer

Heavenly Father, thank You for the woman who raised my husband, loved him, and nurtured him. I recognize there is room in his life for both of us. I release any resentment, anger, or jealousy I may have toward her and ask You to help me love her as You do. I will actively seek a healthy relationship with her, committing to an open heart and a willingness to communicate with her. I will pray for her regularly. Daily, remind me afresh that I am investing in a long-term relationship that will be beneficial to the entire family. Thank You in advance for peace, patience, and the will to pursue a relationship that honors and pleases You. *(Inspired by Col. 1:10; Gal. 5:22–23)*

Chapter 6

I Don't Trust You and You Don't Trust Me!

*H*ere's a brief compilation of what women told us in the survey when it came to the issue of trust.

> "She can be manipulative and uses her influence in my life to get what she wants. She is self-centered, although it may have gotten a little better—as long as she gets what she wants."—MIL

> "She talks about family members behind their backs, and the fact is that if we tell her something, the entire family will know in twenty-four hours."—MIL

> "She rated everything I did, from housework to how I parented my children. I've not felt accepted or good enough. Always judged. Never trusted."—DIL

Unfortunately, there's more. Much more.

Let's first examine the definition of trust and how it's built.

The Burning Question

What is trust?
How do I build it—especially when it's broken?

Trust Is . . .

Trust is reliance on the integrity, strength, ability, and character of a person or thing. To trust is to place confidence in.

You can trust someone when . . .

- You believe the other person has your best interests at heart. She is concerned about and cares for you.
- Your experience is that she is truthful and honest.
- You believe she would not do something to hurt you intentionally or for selfish gain.
- You can rely on the person. Her behavior follows a consistent pattern, and you know what to expect from her.

When these conditions and behaviors are *not* present, it is difficult, if not impossible, to have a relationship based on trust. Sadly, the results of our survey revealed rampant distrust between MILs and DILs.

- Only 48 percent scored their in-law as honest. Less than half!
- About three-fourths (67 percent) rated their in-law as not being a candid person.
- Just 40 percent said the in-law does what is right on a regular basis.
- Some 65 percent rated her as someone who does not trust others.
- Only half (50 percent) rated her as reliable in word and deed.

What could possibly contribute to such dismal responses? Our respondents let us in on that information as well. Following are the issues and behaviors that most often contributed to lack of trust:

- Holds grudges, keeps score, or is unforgiving (32 percent)
- Guarded, secretive, and hard to read (27 percent)
- Blames others (12 percent)
- Cold, aloof, distant, or indifferent (12 percent)
- Dishonest or lying (10 percent)

These numbers make it clear that telling the truth is not the only behavior required in order to build trust with others. The results of relationships where suspicion and mistrust are present are heartbreaking. Those involved in such relationships feel rejected, sad, judged, isolated, and hurt.

Is there a reason why MILs and DILs are so hampered by trust issues? When my sons began to date, I was naturally curious about the girls they were interested in. For the most part, the boys brought them into our home, introduced them, and helped us feel comfortable with them. But they were more guarded about these relationships in their conversations with us than they were on most other topics. It was the first time I found myself thinking, "What have we here? I wonder what he is really feeling about this girl?"

This was the time when our sons began to take the phone into their rooms for long conversations. I knew it was not just one of the guys on the other end of the line. I was vaguely aware of a notebook that got passed back and forth with messages for a special girl. Pants pockets seemed to get cleaned out more thoroughly before being tossed into the hamper.

It was the first time I felt shut out of the lives of my sons. I wasn't hurt by it, nor was I angry. I was just aware that things had changed—shifted a bit in a way I hadn't seen coming. And I felt slightly off-balance with it all.

Some moms feel as though their sons are slipping away. It's natural to guard and protect what you consider *yours*. I've had many conversations in the past year with women who talked about their DILs like she was the "other woman":

- "She's taken him away."
- "She stole him from me."
- "He is mine. He's always going to be mine. She just needs to accept that."

Not necessarily a relationship steeped in trust, is it? While I understand that the transition is tough for some moms, it's *supposed* to happen. If we want what's best for our sons, we must accept that he was ours to raise, but we did so as preparation for the woman who would eventually—and rightfully—have first place in his heart and life.

For many DILs—well, they've seen the movies, watched the comedians, read the books, and learned from the experiences of their mothers, sisters, and friends. It's usually not a positive lesson: prepare yourself—he may be wonderful, but he has a mother. And you will have to deal with her, so you'd better set her straight right from the beginning.

When you've got the shotgun loaded for bear, any movement in the bushes can justify a barrelful of buckshot. A young wife may anticipate that any word from her husband's mom will be soaked in negativity, and the DIL thus becomes unable to hear anything positive. She is over-prepared for criticism, judgment, and unwanted advice, so that even a casual comment may come across like nails on a blackboard. "Oh, the new sofa is big," becomes, "Who in their right mind would choose such a huge, ugly sofa!"

If our experience has taught us to judge our MILs so harshly, how do we move beyond it? As in all things for the Christ-follower, we do it in His Spirit and by the power of His Word. A critical step in synchronizing our steps with His is to recognize where the thoughts and beliefs originate.

Mistrust Is Rooted in Fear

Mistrust will attempt to direct our thoughts and mislead our hearts. When this happens, we should ask ourselves, "What is it I value that I am trying to protect?" At the heart of mistrust is the fear that something we love, something important to us, will be lost or taken from us. Both MILs and DILs have something that is potentially on the line, something at stake. Someone to lose.

When the temptation of fear, suspicion, or mistrust comes over us, we can be certain it does not come from the Father. "For God has not given us a spirit of fear, but of power and of love and of a sound mind" (2 Tim. 1:7 NKJV). We must cast aside such thoughts and choose to think on those things that are pure, lovely, and of a good report.

Could we be fooled or taken advantage of by our in-law if we take this approach? Perhaps. But the alternative is to eliminate the power of the Holy Spirit to guide us in our relationships and in His place rely only on our personal experience. I would rather be fooled and disappointed on occasion because I've trusted God than live with the expectation of betrayal at every step. The impact of not trusting others is significant.

- We are guarded at all times, secretive, and hard to read. Others avoid us as a result.
- Suspicion becomes our approach in each new relationship.
- We become isolated, living with the expectation of hurt or betrayal.
- We have few friends and lack genuine intimacy.
- We automatically assign a bad motive or intent when others let us down.

We all make mistakes. No one is 100 percent reliable. Circumstances sometimes prevent follow-through on a promise. We fail to communicate clearly or completely, which results in misunderstanding. We forget. We get busy. We are human. Stuff happens that can cause us to question the trustworthiness of others, but it's the intent of the heart that should carry weight in our assessments. Was the act intentional? Was it designed to damage or hurt me? If the answer is no, we must offer grace. Even if the answer is yes, we must offer grace. We will need it returned to us, probably sooner than we'd like to believe.

Next, we need to communicate with our in-law about the incident that tempted us to withdraw our trust from her. If we can create a common understanding about the impact of the situation, it will help build an even stronger level of trust in the future. In other words, we need to tell the other person, "What you did hurt me and caused me to lose trust in you." Trust is built when we are open, candid, and honest with one another. It demonstrates *our* trustworthiness. It sends the message, "You are important to me. This relationship is important to me. I was willing to risk my discomfort to discuss this with you, because I know you would want to understand how it made me feel."

Trust is not an add-water-and-stir proposition. It requires time. Trust must prove itself over a period of sustained consistency. Like a checking account, you have to make frequent and consistent deposits so you can draw on it confidently.

The good news is, we have real tools to help us understand how to build trust as well as methods to identify and overcome some traps that can break it. We call them Trust Builders and Trust Busters. When we understand their impact and know how to use them, these behaviors, grounded in God's Word, provide a pattern for cultivating trusting relationships.

Let's first take a look at Trust Builders.

TRUST BUILDERS	SCRIPTURAL FOUNDATION
Honor Your Word • Do what you say you will do. • When unable to keep a commitment, communicate quickly and provide a good reason why. • Ensure that your word is reliable; you will follow through.	"But if you fail to keep your word, then you will have sinned against the Lord, and you may be sure that your sin will find you out" (Num. 32:23).
Own Your Mistakes • Accept responsibility for your actions. • Apologize when you are wrong. • Be self-aware about your own failures and acknowledge them. • Resist blaming others to shift responsibility.	"She fell at his feet and said, 'I accept all blame in this matter, my lord'" (1 Sam. 25:24). "Pride leads to disgrace, but with humility comes wisdom" (Prov. 11:2).
Show Loyalty • Maintain confidentiality; don't betray it. • Defend others when they are not present to defend themselves.	"When arguing with your neighbor, don't betray another person's secret. Others may accuse you of gossip, and you will never regain your good reputation" (Prov. 25:9–10).

Be Consistent
- Make sure people know what to expect from you.
- Live so you have a reliable pattern of behavior, conversation, and expressed values.

"Oh, that my actions would consistently reflect your decrees!" (Ps. 119:5).

"Even children are known by the way they act, whether their conduct is pure, and whether it is right" (Prov. 20:11).

Support the Interests of Others
- Don't be driven by self-interest; refrain from selfishness and self-absorption.
- Support others in action and word, even though it is not your preferred approach.

"Those others do not have pure motives as they preach about Christ. They preach with selfish ambition, not sincerely, intending to make my chains more painful to me" (Phil. 1:17).

"Let each of you look out not only for his own interests, but also for the interests of others" (Phil. 2:4 NKJV).

Tell the Truth
- Be candid but kind.
- Use truth to liberate, not annihilate.

"So stop telling lies. Let us tell our neighbors the truth, for we are all parts of the same body" (Eph. 4:25).

"Speaking the truth in love, [we] may grow up in all things into Him who is the head—Christ" (Eph. 4:15 NKJV).

Trust Others
- Believe that others are essentially honest.
- Trust until given a reason not to.
- Be open and willing to disclose appropriately.

Paul consistently expressed trust in Timothy as well as in the churches he communicated with. It boosted their confidence and served to motivate them.

In chapter 1, we discovered the difference between walking in love versus walking in the law in the DIL/MIL relationship. As you review the Trust Builders, you will see an active display of love in the behaviors described here: honor your word, trust others, show loyalty, etc. The commandment to walk in love found in 2 John 1:6 is a clear indication of the path that pleases our heavenly Father. It is the one Jesus walked out for us. How much more loyalty and trust could God possibly have shown than to send us His Son? Scripture tells us that Jesus *is* the truth, and He placed our interests above His majesty, His power, and His rightful place seated at the Father's right hand when He came to earth as a man to rescue us from the power of sin and death.

When we struggle to consistently demonstrate the loving behaviors required for trust, we need only remember our clear example: the living example of Christ.

Here's an important point to consider: mistrust runs contrary to who we are in Christ. The very nature of our relationship in Christ requires us to trust in that which we cannot see, touch, taste, smell, or hear. Most of us have sensed the presence of Jesus, but few of us would claim to have seen the physical body of Christ or heard an audible voice that we know is His. Life in Him requires trust.

Is trust an easy path to walk fully with Jesus daily? No. Nor will it be easy to trust every person every day. Some make it quite challenging to trust, but someone has to go first. Why not you?

Because *intention* is an important component of trustworthiness, we need to be aware that we may break trust at times without meaning to. Few of us roll out of bed in the morning and say, "Today, I'm going to break trust with someone." For most of us, it's nearly always accidental when it happens.

> I forget a commitment to babysit, and when my DIL calls to say she's on her way, I have to tell her I'm not available.

Work calls me in, and I dash off, leaving my MIL waiting at the café for our lunch date.

Neither example involves any intent to break trust—it's merely an oversight—but the impact on the other person is still the same. And it will remain a problem until communication clears up the incident. Even then, it may still leave a mark if it has become a familiar pattern. Here's the challenge:

- We understand the valid reason for our broken commitment and may assume others are also clear about what prevented us from keeping our word. No conversation is necessary from our point of view.
- We are uncomfortable with letting our in-law know directly how aggravated we are by her behavior, so we tell someone else—and it gets back to her.

I didn't intend to hurt the other person. I didn't intend to break a promise. But I did. If we are honest with ourselves (could we please start there?), we must recognize that we give ourselves extra credit for our good intentions but judge others on their actions. One of the first steps toward creating trusting relationships is demonstrating our own trustworthiness.

So let's take a look at the behaviors that break trust, even if it's not on purpose. We call them Trust Busters, and they, too, have a scriptural foundation.

Trust Busters	Scriptural Foundation
Breaks Confidences • Gossips. • Drops hints about others' private issues. • Requests prayer for others in order to share their story under guise of spirituality.	"As for my companion, he betrayed his friends; he broke his promises. His words are as smooth as butter, but in his heart is war" (Ps. 55:20–21).

Doubts Others

- Believes others pretend to be more honest than they really are.
- Cautious of people until they have demonstrated an extended period of trustworthiness.
- Believes most people will tell a lie to get out of trouble or make themselves look better.

"So you must live as God's obedient children. Don't slip back into your old ways of living to satisfy your own desires. You didn't know any better then" (1 Peter 1:14).

"We're not in charge of how you live out the faith, looking over your shoulders, suspiciously critical. We're partners, working alongside you, joyfully expectant. I know that you stand by your own faith, not by ours" (2 Cor. 1:24 MSG).

Closed to Ideas and Opinions of Others

- Insists on her own way of doing things.
- Quick to dismiss others' ideas because "that won't work" or "we tried that already."

"[Love] does not insist on its own way; it is not irritable or resentful" (1 Cor. 13:5 ESV).

Attempts to Control/Manipulate

- Tries to control or manipulate others for personal gain or private agenda.
- Gives unsolicited advice; offended or hurt if advice is not taken.
- Feels entitled to give opinions liberally.

"So, my very dear friends, when you see people reducing God to something they can use or control, get out of their company as fast as you can" (1 Cor. 10:14 MSG).

"The tools of our trade aren't for marketing or manipulation, but they are for demolishing that entire massively corrupt culture" (2 Cor. 10:3–4 MSG).

Guarded or Secretive
- Discloses little of her life experience, opinions, or feelings.
- Is often quiet during discussion; you never know where she stands on a topic or situation.
- It takes a third party to reveal, to your surprise, that she has bad feelings toward you.

"God will judge us for everything we do, including every secret thing, whether good or bad" (Eccl. 12:14).

"But I, the Lord, search all hearts and examine secret motives. I give all people their due rewards, according to what their actions deserve" (Jer. 17:10).

Dishonest
- Sugarcoats the truth.
- Lies to protect self or self-interest.
- Is "creative" with the truth; uses half-truths, omissions.

"Nevertheless they flattered Him with their mouth, and they lied to Him with their tongue" (Ps. 78:36 NKJV).

"Your sins are telling your mouth what to say. Your words are based on clever deception" (Job 15:5).

Keeps Score or Holds Grudges
- Has long memory for past hurts and conflicts.
- Brings up issues from the past when dealing with today's challenges.
- Says things like, "I will never forget that you . . ." or, "I will never forgive you for . . ."

"When you stand praying, if you hold anything against anyone, forgive them, so that your Father in heaven may forgive you your sins" (Mark 11:25 NIV).

"Bear with each other and forgive one another if any of you has a grievance against someone. Forgive as the Lord forgave you" (Col. 3:13 NIV).

These are the Trust Busters to avoid. Regardless of how good our intentions may be, if we operate in one or more of these Trust Busters, we will damage trust, and the opportunity for solid relationships evaporates.

What if you are already in a "trust hole"? What if suspicion is on the rise and the relationship already suffers from lack of trust?

Repairing trust is certainly a tougher task than building it. Rebuilding a person's trust requires time, sometimes a very long time. Depending on the depth of the hurt or perceived betrayal, you or the other person may feel hesitant to trust again. "Fool me once, shame on you. Fool me twice, shame on me," is the rationale. Some people desire to restore relationship and seem to forgive and move on more quickly, based on their belief that everyone makes mistakes. The experience your WIL has had with extending trust to others after hurt will also be a factor. You may be at the mercy of her previous experiences, even if they did not involve you personally.

Consistency in your actions and behaviors is the key to regaining the trust of another. If you are the offending party, the one who broke the trust, you have no right to demand or expect trust to be restored. You can only prove by what you say and what you do, coupled with patience and perseverance, that you can once again be trusted. Confidence in you comes when you are consistent in your character.

A good place to start is to identify which of the Busters is the culprit and address it with a Builder.

- Have you broken a confidence or gossiped? Use the Trust Builder "Own Your Mistakes." Apologize and ask for forgiveness.
- Been holding a grudge or keeping score? The Builder "Tell the Truth" can help you repair it. 'Fess up, come clean, and eliminate the scoreboard.
- Are you attempting to control or manipulate? Remember, this is not Burger King and you can't always have it your way. Use the Builder "Support the Interests of Others."

What if the offending party doesn't step up to repair the relationship? Are you willing to make the first move? Let's look at the story of Donna and Tammy.

Darren and Tammy were very young—both only nineteen—when they sought the blessing of Darren's mom, Donna, and his dad to marry. Although they liked Tammy, they declined. They felt the couple was too young and withheld their blessing. Donna was fearful that the marriage would end in divorce.

Darren and Tammy then enlisted the help of others, including some of Tammy's family members. They planned a wedding in another community. Donna and her husband were not invited and were not aware of the marriage until after the fact. They were deeply hurt.

Despite their disappointment and the early challenges in the relationship, Darren's parents decided on and demonstrated a loving and inclusive approach with Tammy. They were aware there had been problems in her home as she grew up, and they made a determined effort to love her into the family. Darren's parents reached out to Tammy and provided both emotional and physical help when Darren served overseas.

Tammy and Darren have been married for six years, and Donna has been impressed by the couple's devotion to one another. She came to understand how committed they are to a successful marriage and was grateful to see them growing in God together.

Donna believed she and her husband had been successful in building a positive and healthy relationship with Tammy. That is, until a friend reported to Donna that Tammy had been posting really ugly things about her on a social media site. When Donna reviewed the comments herself, she was shocked, angry, and hurt. She confronted Tammy, who responded with anger and no real explanation. Although Donna was unaware of it, the family has been disrupted with a six-year-long rift—the entire life of the young couple's marriage.

It certainly sounds as though Tammy owes Donna an apology. So far, that has not been forthcoming. Donna has felt helpless and hopeless in the situation and waits for her daughter-in-law's request for forgiveness. But Donna is *not* without options. There is much she can do to bridge this gap and help reconcile this relationship and this family *if* she is willing to do it.

I suggested that Tammy originally felt rejected by Darren's family when they wanted to marry. Rejection was something she had experienced with her own family growing up. "You are not wanted. You are not good enough for our son. You are not welcome here," was the message she heard, although it was not the one spoken or intended. Those words had taken on a life of their own, and Tammy has stewed in them for six years and probably added to them in her heart. "We don't accept you as family."

Donna should consider speaking to Tammy to let her know that although she and Darren's dad had been unwilling to bless the marriage, they can see how good Tammy and Darren are together. She could do the following:

- Apologize for the hurt that has been caused.
- Ask Tammy for forgiveness.
- Ask Tammy to understand that she was never the issue—it was the couple's age.
- Tell Tammy how grateful she is that her son chose her—that his family can clearly see how devoted to one another they are and how happy her son is.

Does it sound like Tammy is off the hook for her bad behavior? Perhaps. But someone has to blink. If Donna makes that choice, she will have cleared the path for God's Spirit to work in Tammy's heart. And Donna will have given Tammy great reasons to build a trusting relationship in the future.

Will Donna take that path? I'm not sure. But it is a choice she can make.

What choice will *you* make when it comes to building trust? Whether you are just beginning a new role as a DIL or a MIL, or whether you are trying to rescue a longtime relationship where trust has been broken, use this simple anagram to remind you that there are tools that can help with the trust-building process.

TIPS

T— Treat her as a family member. She is connected to someone you love dearly.

R—Release her. Set grudges aside and forgive her for past
hurts.

U—Use the Word as your guide. Speak the truth in love.

S— Set aside personal agendas. Avoid attempting to control
or manipulate.

T— Trust her; give trust in order to gain it.

You get the idea. So let's spend a minute or two identifying
where you are on a scale that will measure how likely you are to
trust others.

SELF-ASSESSMENT: How Willing Am I to Trust Others?

Circle the numbers that best represent the strength of your beliefs about each statement. Use the directions below to determine your score.

BELIEFS	Strongly Disagree	Somewhat Disagree	Slightly Disagree	Slightly Agree	Somewhat Agree	Strongly Agree
1. I believe most people are generally trustworthy.	1	2	3	4	5	6
2. Most people pretend to be more honest than they really are.	6	5	4	3	2	1
3. I usually give acquaintances the benefit of the doubt if they do something selfish or self-serving.	1	2	3	4	5	6
4. My typical approach is to be cautious of people. They have to earn trust with me over time; I don't automatically give it.	6	5	4	3	2	1
5. Most people would lie if it would get them out of a difficult situation or make them look better to others.	6	5	4	3	2	1
6. I tend to trust people pretty quickly, even if we've just met for the first time.	1	2	3	4	5	6
7. Most people can be counted on to follow through and do what they say they will do.	1	2	3	4	5	6
8. Unless you remain aware, people will take advantage of you to improve their position or gain an advantage over you.	6	5	4	3	2	1

YOUR SCORE:
Add all the circled numbers. Mark the sum on the scale below.

LEVEL OF TRUST

| 1 | 5 | 10 | 15 | 20 | 25 | 30 | 35 | 40 | 45 | 48 |

1–8 = LOW   9–20 = MODERATE   21–35 = HIGH   36–48 = VERY HIGH

PLAN OF ACTION
I Will Trust You, and You Can Trust Me!

Review the tips from this chapter as well as your self-assessment score. Use this information to help guide you as you respond to the questions below.

Which of the TRUST BUILDERS will you commit to demonstrating?

- ☐ Honor Your Word
- ☐ Own Your Mistakes
- ☐ Show Loyalty
- ☐ Be Consistent
- ☐ Support the Interests of Others
- ☐ Tell the Truth
- ☐ Trust Others

Which of the TRUST BUSTERS will you commit to eliminating?

- ☐ Breaks Confidences
- ☐ Doubts Others
- ☐ Closed to Ideas and Opinions of Others
- ☐ Attempts to Control/Manipulate
- ☐ Guarded or Secretive
- ☐ Dishonest
- ☐ Keeps Score or Holds Grudges

What were the three key points that spoke to your heart in this section?

_____
_____
_____
_____
_____
_____

Stop for a moment and ask the Lord to reveal to you any lessons He desires to add to your understanding.

_____
_____
_____
_____
_____
_____

Write out your action plan.

- WHAT will you do?

_____

_____

_____

_____

_____

_____

- HOW will you do it? (Identify the specific steps.)

_____

_____

_____

_____

_____

_____

_____

_____

_____

- WHEN will you start? (A goal is a dream with a deadline!)

_____

_____

What Would Ruth and Naomi Do?

The word _trust_ stands out in this chapter. How did Ruth and Naomi show trust with one another? Ruth entrusted her life into Naomi's hands, leaving her own homeland to go with Naomi to the place of her birth. Naomi trusted Ruth to find a way to provide for their needs. They operated in a form of mutual surrender to each other. Even when Naomi's strategy to gain the favor of Boaz and secure a commitment to provide for them seemed odd and certainly unfamiliar, Ruth trusted Naomi and went along with her plan. Sometimes we have to trust others, putting aside our own agenda for the greater good of the relationships we hold dear.

Prayer

Father, You trusted a sinful world with the most precious of gifts: Your only Son, Jesus. Thank You for Your demonstration of giving trust where it was unwarranted and undeserved. I trust You first and know You will open my heart to build (or rebuild) trust as I surrender my relationship with my WIL to You. I seek You in this matter and know You will show me the right path. I will use the tools You've provided me in Scripture, and I will with consistency, patience, and perseverance demonstrate them in my relationship. I ask that You strengthen me to accomplish this and ask for Your help in hearing the voice of Your Spirit guiding me in this commitment. Thank You for the power of Your Word working in my life on this issue. *(Inspired by Prov. 3:4–7)*

Chapter 7

Can We Get There from Here?
Bridging the Communication Gap

*T*hings got uncomfortable very quickly after the wedding planning began. I knew she wasn't crazy about me, but she had never been rude," Rita explained. "I was so upset the night she and my son announced their engagement. We were completely blindsided—not a word to us, although apparently her parents knew all about it. I was stunned to hear about it in a room full of people.

"When I asked about their plans, she let me know in no uncertain terms she didn't need my help with the wedding planning. I wasn't trying to butt in; I was just interested. It felt like a warning of things to come: stay out of the planning and out of our lives."

Her daughter-in-law's version of the experience was significantly different. "Eric is an only child, and I think she had been dreading this day. I'm sure she thinks of our wedding as the day she will lose her son. But she did try to put her best face forward when we announced our engagement," recalls Amber. "She smiled and congratulated us—what else could she do with everyone at the restaurant? But it was evident she was not happy about being surprised with our news. She told Eric's sister she felt ambushed—that we had purposely announced it in public so she couldn't make a scene. Even if it's partially true, it really ticked me off when I heard it. And almost immediately, she tried to inject herself into the wedding, asking a bunch of questions."

The situation continued to breed animosity between the two women, each venting to others in the family and often to the groom himself. Eric felt caught in the middle of the conflict. He agreed Amber was rough on his mom, but he also knew Rita could be quite controlling. It wasn't long before all direct communication came to a halt, with both the bride-to-be and the mother of the groom using Eric as a go-between when information needed to be exchanged. There were lots of angry words and more than a few tears, with Eric trying to patch things up before the big day. He was not successful, and the silence continues. Rita and Amber are both waiting for the other to apologize. It doesn't appear that's going to happen anytime soon.

The Burning Question

**How can we do this communication thing better?
Can we bridge the gap?**

In the research done for this book, we surveyed women-in-law about their communication with one another. Sixty percent said they have *never* had a successful candid conversation with their WIL dealing with their differences in an effort to improve the relationship. Sixty-nine percent said they had never even attempted to have that conversation! Several identified characteristics in the other woman that made communication difficult, including these:

- opinionated
- manipulative
- shuts down
- judgmental
- argumentative
- holds grudges

- highly critical
- unforgiving
- unreasonable
- controlling
- won't listen
- angry

The survey responses paint a clear picture: we don't do this communication thing well. Some of the comments that were most hurtful included one mother-in-law who said to her son's wife, "Don't forget, dear, wives come and go. I will always be his mother."

When asked to respond to the question, "What's the most important conversation you've had with your in-law?" there were many discouraging responses.

> "There *is* no conversation. She doesn't like confrontation, and she becomes very abrasive and combative with me."

> "I can't recall a conversation about anything of significance, because I stopped talking to her about anything but the mundane."

> "I don't believe there has ever been even one."

But there were some encouraging responses as well:

> "Very early on in our relationship she kindly but firmly pointed out my role in a quarrel with another family member, and although she was kind, she was direct, and it helped me see the error of my ways."

> "After several months of difficult conversations, she and I decided that we were going to make a drastic change. Both of us have watched as previous generations have had hard mother/daughter-in-law relationships and we decided we didn't want that to be true of us. We also decided we did not want my children growing up with a negative idea of in-laws."

> "We've gone through things over the past few years, but prayer, communication, and transparency have allowed us to work through the tough times."

> "The most important conversation was when we decided we were on the same side. We established that we were going to recognize Satan as one who comes to steal, kill, and destroy and that is what he

was trying to accomplish in our relationship. We agreed on boundaries and rules and agreed to hold each other accountable to our new standard. That was eighteen months ago, and our relationship is wonderful!"

So there is hope. As you can see from the last three responses above, there was a recognition that things needed to change in order for the relationship to have any chance of being healthy. These women made intentional choices about their WIL relationships and figured out how to communicate in an effective way.

Communication is tricky business. Talking is easy, but genuine communication is not. So how is communication defined? *It is the transmission of a message in a manner that enables both parties to have a shared understanding of what has been said.* In other words, we assign the same meaning to the words spoken. Rita and Amber walked away from that engagement party with clear messages, but they were different in their interpretation. And so the drama began.

There are other contributing factors at play that can short-circuit our conversation. As we learned in the previous chapter, our experiences shape how we see and hear things. If trust is not present, we listen between the words for things unsaid, attaching meaning to every tilt of the head, tone of voice, and twitch of the brow. The result of this type of interpretation often sounds something like, "Well, I know you *said* you'd keep the kids for me, but it was clear to me you didn't want to!"

Once we begin to operate on assumption, conflict can occur. For many, conflict is so uncomfortable that we decide to forego the conversation entirely in order to keep the peace. Silence is not peace. It's avoidance, and it's one of the most cavernous and damaging places to find yourself. Although Rita and Amber have cut off all communication, the conflict is alive and well. It's just unspoken. They talk about it—just not to one another.

Most of us lack knowledge and instruction on communicating effectively, so we sit on our feelings, letting our thoughts and concerns go unexpressed. Unexpressed, that is, until we can no longer maintain the silence and blow up, often in dramatic and unproductive ways. Then we just create a greater problem, as words expressed in anger are often ugly and damaging. "It's not the vented pot that blows its lid," my mom used to say. "It's the one with the lid screwed on too tight that eventually explodes." Smart lady, my mom.

So how do you open the lines of communication? How do you establish good communication if the relationship is not in turmoil but is less open, candid, and comfortable than you'd like it to be? As in anything you'd like to build, you need some tools. Let's learn to speak the truth in love.

SPEAK is an easy acronym to help us remember that communication requires skill in order to create a peaceful process with a peaceable result.

S—Seek permission to have the discussion.

P—Present the issue, concern, or idea.

E—Explore solutions and ask questions.

A—Acknowledge what you hear.

K—Keep focused on the present, not past history.

Let's take a look at each of these components.

Seek Permission to Have the Discussion

Have you ever walked in the door after work, arms filled with groceries, mail tucked under one arm, only to find someone waiting to pounce on you the minute you set foot in the door, wanting to discuss an important issue? *Not now!* our brain screams. It's just not the right time. We're not in the best frame of mind for discussing anything more important than finding a flat place to set down those bags.

Timing, as they say, is everything. It's an important component of successful communication. If you deliver the right message at the wrong time, you will often be disappointed with the result. You never know what the other person's day has been like or whether they are struggling with something that makes this a bad time for a conversation. I have a wonderful friend who always asks when I pick up the phone, "Hi. I wanted to talk with you about our holiday plans. Is this a good time?" In other words, *she seeks permission* before launching ahead, allowing me to commit to the conversation or suggest an alternate time. Her approach is respectful of my life, my time, and my mind-set at the moment. And it sets the stage for successful communication.

This is especially true in the world of electronics we live in today. E-mail, text messages, and phones are all convenient methods of staying in touch. But they are blind to what's happening in the life of the person on the other end of the line. We simply pick up that device and start "talking." I've received texts in the middle of dinner, and if no immediate response is given, I get a "HELLO???" I've been guilty of doing that myself. We've come to believe we're entitled to communicate with another person at any time we choose, that it's our right. But it's not. *Seek permission* and start off with mutual readiness.

If there has been a conflict or a time of silence over an upset, be specific when you seek permission. "I'd like to talk with you about the upcoming Christmas holidays. Last year seemed to be a challenge. I think it might help if we discussed it well ahead of time and put a plan together so we can eliminate some of the stress we experienced when we tried to work out the details. Would this be a good time for us to talk?"

Present the Issue, Concern, or Idea

Once both of you have committed to the conversation, the next step is to present information. For example, you might:

- Share information, ideas, or thoughts on the topic you want to discuss.
- Identify a concern you want to address and explaining why it's a concern for you.

- Disclose an opinion or perspective on an issue, opportunity, or event.

This is your opportunity to begin the conversation by clearly explaining what you think or feel needs to be expressed.

Have you ever found yourself wondering, ten minutes into a conversation, "What's she rambling on about? I can't even follow her train of thought. If she has a point, I wish she'd just get to it, please." We wear people out when we fail to organize and express our thoughts effectively so they can participate in the conversation in a meaningful way. Sometimes it's uncomfortable to get down to business, so we try to work up to it or back into it. Don't.

Be straightforward and clear in the information you present. Don't beat around the bush, as it requires others to fill in the gaps with their own assumptions. Assumptions create a shaky foundation when it comes to building good communication.

Your conversation might sound something like this: "Mom, Dave and I have discussed the possibility of flying east to be with my family for Christmas this year. We've always celebrated with you, Dad, and all of the rest of Dave's family in your home. We've loved being together. You've always made the holidays special with all of your traditional touches—the baking, the decorating—the house is so alive at Christmas. You've always included my folks in the invitation, but as my dad's health has declined, it's not feasible for them to join us here. The travel is too much for him. My sisters have been upset with me for several years, and last year it became a real point of contention. Last Christmas was pretty stressful for us. I know how much you love hearing the kids sing carols and watching them open their packages and sit with their grandpa for the reading of the Christmas story from the Bible. I've been concerned you'd be upset if we weren't here this year, and I don't want that to happen. I'm missing my folks, and I hope we can work out a plan to celebrate with both families."

This approach makes it clear that you are looking for solutions and a way to address a problem or heal a rift. It's not assigning a motive, blaming, or demanding. You are making a statement of the circumstances *as you experienced them.* Remember, we may not all have the same experience of the same event.

Choose your tone of voice intentionally in this step. It confirms a collaborative (or conciliatory) motive when done well. Any hint of sarcasm will spoil the moment. Sincere, open, and interested are the intentions you want to convey. You are setting a tone that will guide the rest of the interaction. Once established, you are ready to explore solutions together.

Explore Solutions and Ask Questions

Exploring solutions is useful any time a decision, solution, or direction needs to be identified. It's not time to rehash who said what or place blame but to find an outcome you can both support. Remember, don't look back; you're not going that way.

Because the purpose of this step is to move forward together, you want to make this a dialogue—a *two-way* conversation. It could be on topics of any kind:

- Deciding how you will celebrate the holiday as an extended family. Who, what, where, when?
- Discussing a family financial concern or options for a family vacation.
- Sharing concern and desire to move beyond a difficult or hurtful experience or resolving a conflict.

What does exploring solutions and asking questions sound like? Let's continue our example.

"So, Dave and I were thinking that since Christmas is on a Wednesday this year, we could spend the weekend before the holiday with you, Dad, and the rest of the family. We could celebrate on Saturday, the twenty-first. I thought if we arrived on Friday night, we could put the kids to bed in the guest room, then hang their stockings and get everything ready for our own special "Christmas morning." We'd all wake up together, do stockings, and get our traditional breakfast ready while we wait on Susan and Mike to arrive with their families. We could open gifts together, sing the carols, and read the Christmas story, then set up your fabulous Christmas Day dinner. What do you think? What ideas for our time together do you have that might work, given the situation and our decision to fly east?"

As soon as you begin to solicit information from the other person, you've begun to move forward *together*, which is the goal.

One of the challenges in exploring solutions is that we most often prefer our own ideas. We have the greatest confidence in our solutions and feel most comfortable with them. It's important in this phase to remain open to the ideas, suggestions, and possible solutions your WIL offers. In fact, an important step is to solicit those ideas by *asking questions*. You may be surprised at the quality of her ideas, and the best solutions are often a combination. A little bit of yours, a little bit of what she suggests, and voila! You've come up with something neither of you could have dreamed up by yourselves. It's not compromise—it's collaboration, a true sign of effective communication.

There are some bullets to dodge when exploring solutions and asking questions. Let's take a look at a few. Be careful if this sounds familiar: "Well, let me tell you my thoughts about this. First, I think we should call Susan and Mike and tell them what we're planning. Second, we should definitely make plans to get up extra early, because that way we'll have more time together. And instead of doing the Bible story at night . . ." And on, and on, barely coming up for air. Have you ever participated in a conversation like that? It's a verbal marathon. You couldn't get a word in if you wanted to. For many of us, it's such a turnoff that we simply stop listening or trying to join the conversation.

It can be tempting at times to do all the talking, to try to push through your solution by telling your WIL what you think without taking time to hear from her. Telling is one-way communication: I talk, you listen. Don't be a teller; tellers work at the bank. Instead, once you have explored possible solutions by sharing your thoughts and ideas, ask questions to draw your

WIL into the conversation and build a two-way dialogue, which is the purpose of this step. Your goal is to gather ideas and gain insight and understanding into your WIL's perspective, ideas, thoughts, and feelings.

There are two primary types of questions: open and closed. Closed questions are helpful in confirming specific information, as in, "Does the movie start at 6 PM?" or, "Are we still planning to go to lunch after church?" The response is a simple yes or no.

But to build dialogue, use open questions, which require a response that goes beyond a single word or two. When you ask an open question, it suggests, *I want to hear what you think; I'm open to your suggestions.* This can encourage others to share more fully.

Here's a quick tip for question starters:

OPEN QUESTION STARTERS	CLOSED QUESTION STARTERS
What	Is
How	Are
Where	Do, Did, Does
Who	Will
When	Can
Why	Would, Should, Could

Reflecting back to the previous step in our holiday example, you will notice that it ends with two open questions: "What do you think?" and "What ideas for our time together do you have that might work, given the situation and our decision to fly east?" The questions become a natural segue to this portion of the conversation. Here's an example of this step, following our holiday discussion:

"How can we make this work for everyone, Mom? I don't want to miss our time together this year; it means so much to all of us. What are your thoughts so we can all participate?"

Ask a good open question or two and then *stop talking.* When you are silent, it suggests to your WIL that it's her turn to speak. *Listen closely* without interruption; interruption often shuts down conversation. Listening is not merely remaining silent. It requires far more. A great definition for listening is *the willingness to be changed by what you hear.* It requires you to set your own preferences aside and commit to a genuinely open mind and heart. That's not always easy, but it is possible. It's an act of your will and it will entirely change the game.

Some of what you hear may not be what you'd hoped for. She may have other ideas or may express upset or even anger. The challenge is to listen without looking for ways to overcome her objections or become defensive. How do you do that? The next step will help.

Acknowledge What You Hear

One of our most vital human needs is to be heard and understood. Listening, as suggested above, can send the message, "I hear you." Being heard is one-half of the equation; alone it is not sufficient. When working toward creating authentic solutions, we must also communicate, "I understand what you're saying."

Please note, we are not suggesting you must *agree* with what the other person is saying. It's an acknowledgment of what was said that communicates, "I get it. I understand how you see the situation or circumstance and am aware of how you feel about it." That's it. Simple. "I hear you. I get you." It's called empathy and is a surefire way to connect in conversation.

Resist the temptation to judge how your WIL feels. Feelings aren't right or wrong. They just *are*. "But what if she's being immature or selfish? Do I actually give her permission to feel that way?" She doesn't need your permission to feel any certain way, and there is no value in passing judgment. Simply let her know you understand.

Saying, "I understand," however, is not an effective way to use empathy. Most often, "I understand," is met with a quick, "No, you don't." We need to respond in a way that *proves* we get it by identifying the situation or circumstance and the impact or feelings associated with it. So what does this nonjudgmental empathy sound like?

- "Clearly, you are disappointed we will be away for the holidays." (Away for the holidays = situation/circumstance; disappointed = impact/feelings.)
- "It's clear that you are angry about the change in our plans." (Change in plans = situation/circumstance; angry = impact/feelings.)
- "I'm sorry you are upset that we aren't coming down for Bill's birthday." (You're sorry she's upset; you aren't apologizing for not coming.)
- "It sounds as though you are excited about the new house!" (New house = situation/circumstance; excited = impact/feelings.)

Empathy is important any time strong feelings or emotions are expressed, whether positive or negative. Understanding equals connection. It's best to acknowledge what you hear as soon as you hear it. Doing so tells your WIL that you are genuinely listening and that you validate her words and her heart.

Once you've acknowledged her, move back to exploring solutions by asking questions. Start by asking questions such as, "Since we can't be here for Christmas Eve, how would you feel about celebrating on the twenty-second before we leave?" or, "I'm disappointed, too, that we had to change our plans. We hate to miss the party. Is the birthday celebration flexible at all?"

The conversation continues back and forth between exploring solutions and asking questions until some real solutions begin to surface. Once you create a plan, ask one more question—a closed question to confirm that you are both on the same page and in agreement. It will sound something like this:

"Is this something we can both commit to?"

"So can we agree and begin working on making this happen?"

"So is this workable? Can we both be happy with our decision and support it fully?"

You are looking for a yes or no this time. If the answer is no, go back to exploring solutions and asking questions to discuss what's missing or not acceptable. Be patient—you will get there.

This method may seem unnatural or cumbersome when you first begin to use it, but it works. And like anything new, it takes a while to get comfortable with the process. Practice makes it easier to do. So start now!

Keep Focused on the Present, Not the Past

There is one last element to SPEAK—the K, as in, "Keep focused on the present, not past history." This last element is not a step that follows in order, as in the fifth thing on the list you do. Rather, it is a mind-set that must be present throughout the discussion in order for it to produce the results you desire. Think of the upstretched arms of the K as supporting the entire process.

When a current situation is reminiscent of a past experience or pattern, it can be difficult to keep the focus where it needs to be: on the issue at hand, the conversation we're having at the moment. This is especially true if the conversation is an attempt to address or resolve a conflict. The Enemy loves to throw the past into the mix in an attempt to derail the conversation. Be vigilant. Commit to keeping your focus on this issue, rather than dredging up old hurts. "This is what you always do!" or, "Well, let's not forget what happened the last time," will get a reaction, but not one that's productive.

A critical element of forgiveness is the determined commitment to let the offense go. The Lord instructs us to forgive others in the same way we are forgiven by Him: fully, completely, and without bringing it up in every conversation. Aren't you grateful for that kind of forgiveness? Christ's way of forgiveness is to be our pattern, but it's a rough road to travel.

I can recall heading into difficult conversations where resolving conflict and addressing hurt were on the agenda. I often took notes to help me stay on track and not allow myself to get off a positive and peaceful path. I sometimes wrote the letters L-I-G at the top of my notes, which stood for *let it go*. Don't misunderstand: I was addressing the conflict or hurt. But I wasn't bringing into the conversation all of the assorted examples from our history together in order to make my case. If there was a pattern to the problem, I would mention it, but I didn't come equipped to drag out every sin and infraction committed by the other party. It's not the pattern God established for us. Deal with this day, this conversation, this opportunity.

So, there you have it. SPEAK the truth in love. Truth without love is just a set of facts and will rarely be effective in working together toward authentic agreement. There is power in agreement. In Amos 3:3, the Word is clear that without agreement it's nearly impossible to walk through this life together. As two women who love the same man, that must be your daily commitment. You are family. Your family can bring glory to God through the way you do life together. The MIL/DIL relationship is typically so poor that your choice to live it God's way will immediately make you stand out in any crowd. And when people say, "You and your mother-in-law seem to genuinely get along well. Boy, are you lucky," you have the perfect opportunity to share with them that it's not luck, it's God.

There is one more area of communication we need to cover before we wrap up this chapter: electronica. Earlier, I touched on it briefly, but let's take a few minutes for a deeper dive.

I am stunned by what I see posted on Facebook and other social media sites. Families and friends are dealing with private matters or conflicts, taking to the airwaves to make their thoughts known to the world. Some really ugly spats are the result, with other Facebook friends chiming in, rooting for one side or the other, and the conflict widens and involves more people. How is that helpful?

The same is true for conversing through e-mail or texting. Although more private, it's still ineffective. Frankly, I think it's the height of cowardice to communicate over the airwaves about a conflict or anything of a sensitive nature. Technology allows us to hide from the difficult issue, and we may surrender good judgment about what we say and how we say it. People say things to one another electronically that they would never say face-to-face. My concern is that we are losing our ability to manage our conversations and relationships without electronic devices involved.

Remember, please, that a text or e-mail does not have a tone of voice until the reader assigns it one. If trouble is brewing, trust me, the other person will assign the communication the wrong tone more often than not. I recently sent a note to someone who had messaged me several hours earlier. My note said, "Forgive me if I didn't respond as quickly as you expected." I learned later that my sincere request was interpreted to be dripping with sarcasm, as if the real message was, "Well! FOR-GIVE ME if I didn't JUMP THE MINUTE the message arrived!" Not my intention at all, but I still had to deal with the impression my message left and the irritation it caused. Sending an electronic message is intentional, but sometimes the poor outcome is accidental. Don't let your electronica replace real conversations. Pick up the phone. Set a coffee date to have the discussion face-to-face. Doing so will save you a world of problems.

On the next pages you will find some great resources.

Woman-to-Woman Conversation Starters. These will help you begin conversations based on your shared womanhood, not your relationship as family. You may discover something about your WIL you didn't know that reveals a bit more of who she is. Use these conversation starters in any informal setting, simply asking one of the questions and letting the interaction flow naturally. Car trips, waiting room, and lazy Sunday afternoons are all great opportunities.

Bridging the Gap Assessment. Use this to discover your communication strengths (so you can leverage them) as well as your opportunities for improvement (so you can develop these important skills).

Guided Journaling. As in previous chapters, this plan of action allows you to incorporate what you have learned in this chapter.

TIP SHEET
Conversation Starters: Woman-to-Woman

These are a fun way to create casual but informative conversations with your woman-in-law. Choose those that you are curious about, and ask away! Remember to share your responses as well.

Just Between Us Girls

- What was your strangest date ever?
- How did you know when you met your hubby that he was the one for you?
- What was the worst hairstyle you ever had?
- Is it easier or harder to be a girl today than when you were a teenager? Why?
- What gift would you love to receive from the man in your life?
- As a child, what did you want to be when you grew up?
- What one thing would you do over if you had the chance?

Down Memory Lane

- What Halloween costumes do you remember as a kid? How did your family celebrate?
- What are your favorite foods from your childhood?
- Which song reminds you of dancing with your sweetheart in high school?
- What do you still have from childhood?
- What was the most expensive thing you bought as a kid?
- What qualities do you value most in friends?
- Which song would you play in a convertible on a sunny day?
- What were your grandparents' funniest habits?

Gourmet Corner

- What's the most impressive meal you've ever cooked?
- Which celebrity chef would you most like to fix you a meal?
- Do you have any treasured handwritten recipes?
- What's your favorite way to eat chocolate?
- What food festival would you love to attend?
- What's your favorite 'go to' kitchen tool?

Family Edition

- What's your favorite family tradition? How did it start?
- Would you rather live for a week in the past or the future? Why?
- Which famous person would you love to meet? What would you ask him or her?
- What family or school rule would you most have liked to change growing up?
- Who's the first person you ever had a crush on?

SELF-ASSESSMENT: Bridging the Communication Gap

Circle the numbers that best represent the frequency of your behavior for each statement. Use the directions below to determine your score.

BEHAVIORS	Never		Seldom		Occasionally		Frequently
1. I select an appropriate time/place for difficult or sensitive conversations with my WIL.	1	2	3	4	5	6	7
2. I tend to do more of the talking in most of the conversations I participate in.	7	6	5	4	3	2	1
3. I refrain from interrupting so others may finish speaking before I respond.	1	2	3	4	5	6	7
4. I often find I am thinking about what I will say next while others are talking.	7	6	5	4	3	2	1
5. It's challenging for me to be open to others' ideas if I believe I know the best or most productive option.	7	6	5	4	3	2	1
6. I pray before I speak to my WIL on a topic I know may upset her or create conflict if not done well.	1	2	3	4	5	6	7
7. I am willing to accept the ideas of others when good rationale is offered, even if it differs from my original plan.	1	2	3	4	5	6	7
8. I don't believe my WIL is interested in improving our relationship, regardless of what I say or do.	7	6	5	4	3	2	1
9. It's my responsibility to address issues with my WIL that create division, hurt, or are damaging to our relationship.	1	2	3	4	5	6	7
10. I will learn and use the skills necessary to establish and maintain good communication with my WIL.	1	2	3	4	5	6	7

BEHAVIOR FREQUENCY

YOUR SCORE:
Add all the circled numbers. Write the sum in the box:

70–61 Healthy Relationship   40–21 Opportunities for Growth
60–41 Strong Relationship   20–10 Important to Change Behavior

PLAN OF ACTION
Bridging the Communication Gap

Review the tips from this chapter, as well as your self-assessment score. Use this information to guide you as you respond to the questions below.

What were the three key points that spoke to your heart in this section?

_____

_____

_____

_____

_____

_____

_____

_____

Stop for a moment and ask the Lord to reveal to you any lessons He desires to add to your understanding.

_____

_____

_____

_____

_____

_____

_____

Write out your action plan.
- WHAT will you do?

_____

_____

_____

_____

_____

_____

_____

_____

- HOW will you do it? (Identify the specific steps.)

_____

_____

_____

_____

_____

_____

- WHEN will you start? (A goal is a dream with a deadline!)

_____

_____

What Would Ruth and Naomi Do?

Ruth and Naomi discussed their situation openly with one another. They each gave their own ideas and ran through several options before agreeing on the plan: Ruth would work in the field of Boaz. It was Ruth's plan to work there, and it was Naomi's plan for her to go in to Boaz personally. Good results came because of good communication. Each of the women held a key to eventually unlocking the door to the solution. We can't assume we know best without having healthy discussions with our WIL. We only know one-half of the equation unless we bridge the communication gap and share our hearts, our ideas, and our thoughts with one another.

Prayer

Thank You, Father, that You communicate with Your children daily through Your Word and Your Spirit. I desire to follow that same pattern of connection through communication with my woman-in-law. I choose to speak the truth in love. Help me always balance truth and love with my words so she experiences Your love through me. I recognize there is power in agreement; we cannot walk together without it. I will take responsibility for the words of my mouth and will weigh them carefully. Life and death are in the power of the tongue, and I will choose life in this relationship. I ask You to bless my commitment and open the heart of my in-law so she will be receptive and willing to share this path with me. *(Inspired by Eph. 4:15; Prov. 18:21)*

Chapter 8

The Outlaw In-Laws:
Rounding Up Your Posse

*T*here's safety in numbers, as the old saying goes. But what does that mean? The *Cambridge Idioms Dictionary* says it is "something that you say which means if people do something difficult or unpleasant together, they are less likely to get harmed or blamed."[1]

Harmed or blamed. Interesting double-edged sword there. In other words, I'm less likely to be hurt if I do some undesirable task as part of a group. I can't or won't be singled out for blame or consequences, because other people joined me in the process. Sounds like a few family gatherings I've heard about at the in-laws: "Well, if we *all* speak up, they can't ignore us this time. They'll *have* to listen to us. But I'm not gonna do it by myself!"

There's a companion to this idea: "Misery loves company," which translates as, "Somehow it's comforting to know I am not the only one experiencing this pain. It would be terrible to think I'm the only person to ever encounter this awful misery."

That desire to find others on the journey may be the basis for these comments taken from our online survey:

> "I have two sisters-in-law who also become very frustrated with my mother-in-law, and when we're all together, I have to admit that at times we get caught up in bashing our MIL. I do have to say though that it has brought the three of us closer!"

---

1. *Cambridge Idioms Dictionary*, 2nd ed, 2006, s.v. "There's safety in numbers"; cited by The Free Dictionary, http://idioms.thefreedictionary.com/There's+safety+in+numbers.

"The other two DILs and I tend to joke that we never know which one will be on the bottom next week with our MIL."

"I think what bothers me most is if I unknowingly upset or hurt her, it would get discussed with everyone else. This has happened at least twice that I'm aware of and has made it difficult to build relationships with the others. We've been married four years, and I have never felt like a part of his family or feel that they have any real interest in getting to know me."

"Ironically, our relationship with my husband's only brother and his wife has probably grown stronger because of it [the poor relationship with her MIL]. They deal with the same issues with her, and since we were married first, we warned them so they knew what to expect. It softened the blow when it started happening to them."

Or it might have just caused them to come to the marriage ready for a fight, where every lift of the eyebrow or tone of voice is interpreted as an invitation to the fray. What probably seemed like a helpful heads-up might have been the greatest disservice possible.

Selfishly, my human rationale tells me that if it's happening to you too, then I know *I'm* not the problem. It validates my innocence and vindicates my role as the victim.

There's a natural tendency to prefer company on a scary journey. Dorothy took Toto and ended up adding the Scarecrow, the Tin Man, and the Lion to her entourage. Life in a new in-law family can feel a little like landing in Oz: there are customs and rules you don't understand, a cast of characters who are unique (to say the least), and you're clear about not wanting to annoy the folks in charge.

Dorothy and her crew bonded through their mutual experience. She didn't have to convince them to be unhappy with their situations. They were already unhappy. When we have shared experiences with people, we naturally tend to gather together. But what if Dorothy had to rally the troops, sharing her own dissatisfaction and fears in order to pull them into the fold and convince them to join forces with her to seek the great wizard?

That's a perfect analogy for what happens at times in our in-law relationships. One person has a negative experience, a conflict, or a hurt with her in-law. She then works to enlighten and warn others, to convince them that they need to band together for protection. And the posse is born. Sometimes those recruited to the posse may have had similar experiences, sometimes not. But they become convinced that it's important to share the information so together they can isolate this person and insulate themselves from further damage.

❦

The Burning Question

What are the pitfalls of a posse?
What harm could it possibly cause?

This is an equal-opportunity hurt: DILs rally the troops (including their husbands) against their MILs, and MILs actively recruit forces against their DILs. The damage is deep and wide. No one goes unscathed, including the grandchildren, children, siblings, aunts, and uncles. Looking back at her relationship with her mother-in-law, one woman had this to say:

> The children were always jumpy when we were with my mother-in-law. The little ones cried and fussed. I think it was the tension between us—they could sense it, even though they didn't understand it. As they got older, they complained about going to visit their grandparents and often we let them stay home. I regret that now. My problem with my mother-in-law cost them their relationship with their dad's family. At the time, it felt good, like they were choosing me. It hurt my husband, though, and they missed out on the special grandma and grandpa stuff I had as a

kid. My MIL accused me once of turning the kids against her. I denied it, but in all candor, I never did anything to encourage their relationship with her or my father-in-law, who was never anything but good to me. He got caught in all that crossfire.

Family members often feel loyal to one party, and the only way to remain so is to follow the rule that says your enemy is my enemy. A person need not have any actual personal negative experience or interaction with that "enemy"; the testimony of the WIL is sufficient.

If Satan can divide the family, he can divide the church. I'm not talking about the local church congregation; I'm referring to the body of Christ. The Lord makes clear that the Enemy's mission is to kill, steal, and destroy. The family is the heart of the church, which makes our relationships a target.

Let's explore the Word of God for insight and understanding in this important relationship and identify the principles supported by Scripture.

Don't Expect Non-Christians to Behave in a Christlike Manner

One of the questions in our survey asked if the relationship had changed over time. Nearly 60 percent said it had improved, and the primary reason given was, "My WIL came to faith in Christ." It shouldn't be a surprise, but many women fail to weigh the impact of an unsaved WIL when dealing with her difficult behavior. When the WIL came to faith, the change was dramatic. "My MIL and I pray together for the family and have done some Bible studies together. It's amazing—I didn't know it could be like this," said one DIL.

Prayer is more appropriate and more in alignment with your Christian walk than gathering reinforcements. Your woman-in-law is related to you through the man-in-the-middle and has influence in your life and that of your family. You have something at stake here personally. More importantly, you are called by the Lord to stand in the gap and pray for her salvation. "But you are the ones chosen by God, chosen for the high calling of priestly work, chosen to be a holy people, God's instruments to do his work and speak out for him, to tell others of the night-and-day difference he made for you—from nothing to something, from rejected to accepted" (1 Peter 2:9–10 MSG).

Be Jesus with skin on for your woman-in-law. Walk out your faith rather than trying to talk her into the kingdom. I don't recall where I first heard it, but it's one of my favorite quotes: "Preach at all times; use words if necessary."

God Does Not Exempt Us from Demonstrating Christlike Behavior in This Relationship

All of the Scripture given to us on godly conduct applies. Love one another. Love those who despitefully use you (take advantage of you). Bless those who curse you. Love your enemy. As we've said earlier, love is not a feeling. It's an intentional choice to be obedient to God's Word in our behavior and speech.

Speaking of speech, let's chat about gossip. It's the fuel of the posse. Do not gossip. Period. That's what happens every time you share a conversation, conflict, or incident with another person, including family members, about your WIL that is critical, slanderous, or dishonoring. The Bible has a lot to say about this subject:

> "A gossip betrays a confidence, but a trustworthy person keeps a secret." (Prov. 11:13 NIV)

> "A perverse person stirs up conflict, and a gossip separates close friends." (Prov. 16:28 NIV)

> "The words of a gossip are like choice morsels; they go down to the inmost parts." (Prov. 18:8 NIV)

> "A gossip betrays a confidence; so avoid anyone who talks too much." (Prov. 20:19 NIV)

And that's just the book of Proverbs! In the first chapter of Romans, Paul lumps gossips in with a nefarious crew—those filled with envy, murder, strife, deceit, and malice. And in the second letter to the church at Corinth he decries, "I fear that there may be discord, jealousy, fits of rage, selfish ambition, slander, *gossip*, arrogance and disorder" (2 Cor. 12:20 NIV; emphasis added). According to the Bible, gossip is a big deal.

The entire thirteenth chapter of 1 Corinthians describes love in clear terms: "Love is patient, love is kind. It does not envy, it does not boast, it is not proud. It does not dishonor others, it is not self-seeking, it is not easily angered, it keeps no record of wrongs. Love does not delight in evil but rejoices with the truth. It always protects, always trusts, always hopes, always perseveres. Love never fails" (1 Cor. 13:4–8 NIV).

If loving Christ's way were easy, there would not be nearly an entire chapter devoted to defining it. Loving those who love us and are good to us, demonstrating care and concern for us, is easy. Loving the unlovely? That's tough, but we are empowered to do all things through Christ. He will strengthen us for each thing He asks us to do. Try saying the verses above out loud, substituting the word "I" each time in place of the word *love* or *it*, as in "I am patient, I am kind, I am not easily angered," and so on. It's a powerful affirmation of your intent and commitment to love.

Here's one last favorite scriptural exhortation before we move toward the resource section. It says it all in very plain terms: "Clean house! Make a clean sweep of malice and pretense, envy and *hurtful talk*. You've had a taste of God. Now, like infants at the breast, drink deep of God's pure kindness. Then you'll grow up mature and whole in God" (1 Peter 2:1–3 MSG; emphasis added). Mature and whole in God—now that's a good promise.

Chapter 7 is a great place to begin again with your WIL. The communication steps will be helpful in communicating openly and honestly. You may ask, "What if she doesn't accept her share of the responsibility? What if I'm the only one willing to work on the relationship? What if she's not open to starting over?"

Sometimes God doesn't change your situation because He's trying to change your heart. Remember, you are not responsible for your WIL's response to your love. You are only responsible to love. Somebody's got to go first. Why not you? You do your part, and let God work on her heart.

Let's look at some resources to help get you started.

TIP SHEET
Avoiding the Pitfalls of the Posse

Select the tips that best fit your situation. Some are focused on improving the relationship if that is your challenge. Others are focused on maintaining the relationship if it's healthy.

Maintain a Good Relationship

- If your WIL is a woman of faith, ask her to help you create a family prayer list for the two of you to share. Meet or speak on the phone at least once or twice a month to pray together.
- Address any upset with your WIL quickly and avoid the temptation to discuss it with other family members. The exception to this rule is a conversation with the man-in-the-middle, if it's appropriate, making sure you're seeking counsel, not recruiting reinforcements.
- Make a point of affirming your WIL for the things she contributes to your life and the life of your family. Is she a great cook? Is she the family prayer warrior? Does she work hard in her career or home? Point it out. Brag on her to others.
- Pray for your woman-in-law daily. For salvation if needed, for growth in God, for health, for anything she shares with you, or as the Spirit of the Lord leads.

Improving the Relationship

- Use the Plan of Action to detail what steps you will take as a result of the information in this chapter.
- Prayerfully approach your WIL and ask if she is willing to speak with you regarding your desire to improve the relationship. Share as God leads you, seeking forgiveness if appropriate, whether she is a Christ-follower or not. Affirm that you are committed to moving forward, putting the past behind you.
- Take to the Lord the hurts, upsets, and grievances in your relationship with your WIL. Ask Him for the comfort you may have sought from others in the past. Release your WIL, forgiving her as God has forgiven you. Ask God to bless her.
- When others speak negatively to you about your WIL, stop them, letting them know you are not willing to participate in the conversation. Ask them to refrain from including you in this type of conversation in the future.
- Make 1 Corinthians 13 a regular part of your personal Bible reading or personal devotion time. Challenge yourself on each point in verses 5–8, using them as a checkup by asking yourself, "Am I demonstrating this with my WIL?"

TIP SHEET
Words Worth Practicing!

Words have a life of their own; once they've been delivered, they have a presence. We can encourage, exhort, or wound with the words of our mouths. When we wound, we need to step in to help the healing process. Here are some suggestions for choosing life and peace when words have gone astray.

When You've Made a Mistake or Created a Conflict, Hurt, or Misunderstanding	When Your WIL Has Made a Mistake or Created a Conflict, Hurt, or Misunderstanding
I'm sorry.	Thank you for your apology.
I was wrong.	Please don't worry about it.
Please forgive me.	I make mistakes too.
	Don't give it another thought.
	It's not a big deal.
	We can fix this.
	I forgive you.

SELF-ASSESSMENT: Am I Rounding Up the Posse?

Circle the numbers that best represent the frequency of your behavior for each statement. Use the directions below to determine your score.

	Strongly Disagree		Disagree		Somewhat Agree		Strongly Agree
1. I have excluded my WIL from family events; it's just not worth the drama.	7	6	5	4	3	2	1
2. I think it's important to warn others about my WIL so they will not be hurt or upset by her behavior.	7	6	5	4	3	2	1
3. It's my responsibility to make the effort to improve this relationship with my WIL.	1	2	3	4	5	6	7
4. I am called to love my WIL, even if she does not demonstrate love toward me.	1	2	3	4	5	6	7
5. I have influenced others to view my WIL in a negative way.	7	6	5	4	3	2	1
6. I pray for my WIL and for our relationship to be healthy and God-honoring.	1	2	3	4	5	6	7
7. The relationship between my WIL and I has caused pain or upset to the man-in-the-middle (son or husband).	7	6	5	4	3	2	1
8. As a Christian, I am called to follow Scripture in my relationship with my WIL. Failing to do so is disobedience to God.	1	2	3	4	5	6	7
9. Holidays, birthdays, and family gatherings are negatively impacted by the tension between my WIL and me.	7	6	5	4	3	2	1
10. I refuse to listen to others speak poorly about my WIL, letting them know I am not willing to participate in such negative conversations.	1	2	3	4	5	6	7

YOUR SCORE:
Add all the circled numbers. Write the sum in the box:

70–61 Healthy Relationship   40–21 Opportunities for Growth
60–41 Strong Relationship   20–10 Important to Change Behavior

PLAN OF ACTION
Retiring your Posse

Review the tips from this chapter as well as your self-assessment score. Use this information to help guide you as you respond to the questions below.

What were the three key points that spoke to your heart in this section?

_____

_____

_____

_____

_____

_____

_____

_____

Stop for a moment and ask the Lord to reveal to you any lessons He desires to add to your understanding.

_____

_____

_____

_____

_____

_____

_____

_____

Write out your action plan.
- WHAT will you do?

_____

_____

_____

_____

_____

_____

_____

- HOW will you do it? (Identify the specific steps.)

_____

_____

_____

_____

_____

_____

_____

- WHEN will you start? (A goal is a dream with a deadline!)

_____

_____

What Would Ruth and Naomi Do?

Ruth could have easily teamed up with Orpah when their husbands died to look after their own best interests, working against Naomi. Ruth didn't leave like Orpah did—she stuck with what she believed was the right thing to do. Ruth didn't go running to her family to create drama by sharing her sob story. What can we learn from her example for our own situations when things haven't happened as we'd hoped or expected? Instead of singing a somebody-done-me-wrong song to a support team who will cheer us on in our stinking thinking, we can follow Ruth's example to deal directly with our WIL, which will always provide a better result.

Prayer

Father, I ask You to guide me in my desire and commitment to honoring You as I honor this relationship in my life. I release my WIL from past hurts and forgive her fully as You have forgiven me. I desire to build a healthy relationship with her and am willing to do whatever is necessary to follow Your leading. I will look for ways to include her, affirm her, and encourage her. I will refrain from discussing her with others in any way that dishonors the role she holds in my life. I surrender my heart to You and ask You to protect it as I move toward a godly relationship with her. Reveal to me anything You desire me to change. Help me pursue peace with my WIL and contribute to our mutual up-building. _(Inspired by Prov. 16:28, Rom. 14:19)_

Chapter 9

Hey Guys! Don't Just Stand There, Do Something!

*W*hen I travel, I take my seat on the plane and quickly bury my face in a book or magazine. It's my "I'm not interested in conversation" signal. I will usually sneak in a quick hello or smile over the top of my book, just to reassure the other person that I'm not creepy while indicating I choose silence.

I broke that rule recently. It turned out to be an aggravating choice.

The young woman who sat down in the center seat beside me smiled as she settled in. In her hand, she clutched a faith-based book by a familiar author. We struck up a conversation about the book, and eventually I shared that I, too, am a writer.

She inquired about my writing, so we talked about this book and about the relationship between mothers-in-law and daughters-in-law.

She sat forward a bit. "I don't have a *bad* relationship with my mother-in-law, but it's not close. That's okay, though. My husband's not close to her either," she added quickly. "We're both really close to my mom and dad. We live about a mile apart, so that's really great."

Uh huh, I thought. *For your folks it's great.*

She went on to explain that her husband's parents were older than hers by about ten years. "And my mother-in-law is just not very, uh—smart. She doesn't enjoy reading, so she just knows what other people tell her or what she sees in the headlines of the *Enquirer* at the grocery store."

I began wishing I hadn't opened this can of worms. I could feel my teeth grind a bit.

"She always acts as though she knows everything, but she doesn't, 'cause you know, she just watches TV. And she's such a worrier, she's always got something new to be anxious about."

"It must be difficult for her," I offered. "To live with so much fear."

"Yeah, I guess. But it's her own choice."

Ugh. Is it too late to change my seat? I thought. *Where is the compassion?*

The woman seemed to have no awareness of the isolation or pain her MIL might be experiencing. She never considered her mother-in-law's heartbreak of having a son who has made the choice to join his wife's family at the expense of his own—never looking back. They live only two hours apart. "We don't see them often," she informed me. "There's nothing to do in their little town, and when you're not interested in just sitting around, talking to them, it isn't worth the drive. They rarely come up to see us either. It takes them at least four hours to make the drive. They're just so slow."

I was tired. It had been a long week. I simply did not have the energy to educate this young woman on the danger of ignoring one of the Big Ten. There was no honor in her heart for his parents.

Clueless. Without. A. Single. Clue.

While I found her attitude disturbing, my real upset was reserved for her husband. How on earth could a Christian man so easily dismiss his parents? How could he abandon them in favor of his wife's younger, apparently more interesting, faster-moving parents?

The Burning Question

What is my role in helping the man-in-the-middle take the lead? How do I do it?

He's the MIM—the man-in-the-middle. And he's not alone when it comes to choosing his wife as the most important woman in his life. He's not wrong to choose his wife. He is terribly wrong in choosing his wife at the expense of not honoring the woman who gave birth to him and raised him well enough that some other woman wanted to spend her life with him. That's not *our* opinion. That's what God has to say on the subject.

Before we married, my fiancé had been serving a dual role in his mother's life. He was her son and, in many ways, the believing head of the household, as his stepdad had not yet come to the Lord. His mom and younger sister depended on him in ways not typical in most homes. Candidly, I had mixed feelings about his level of family responsibility. On the one hand, I was proud of him. On the other, the circumstances required more from him than I was sometimes willing to invest.

Things came to a head the night of my birthday. My hubby-to-be and I had selected my engagement ring, and this was our night to celebrate. He was going to place the ring on my finger at dinner in a special restaurant. But when he arrived to pick me up, it was clear that something was amiss.

"Babe," he said as he pulled me into the living room. "I'm afraid we are going to have to wait a couple of weeks for your ring." He looked forlorn, and I was stunned.

"Didn't the jeweler have it ready?" I asked.

"No, it's ready. But my mom needed some help with the utility bills, and I didn't have the money to pay the balance on your ring after I helped her out." He held my hand tightly. I pulled it from his grip and proceeded to pitch a fit. After a moment or two, my mother appeared in the living room entrance. She looked at me squarely.

"May I have a word with you, Deb?"

"Not now, Mom. We're in the middle of something here."

"Yes. I know. I need to speak with you. Now," she insisted.

I huffed my way into the kitchen where she waited. Her voice was calm but firm. "Any man who would take such good care of his mother would certainly take great care of his wife." She went on. "If you're too immature to see that, perhaps you don't deserve him." And then she exited the kitchen, leaving me with my mouth hanging open.

She was right. I had been shortsighted. He was taking appropriate care of his mother, and I responded with an astonishing level of selfish immaturity. That moment was my introduction to understanding that a husband deserves to have a relationship with both his mother and his wife, without having to referee on a regular basis. There is room for us both without making him the man-in-the-choke-hold.

The MIM doesn't necessarily choose to be the guy covering both first and third bases at the same time. The women in his life often assign him that role, and they do it for all the reasons we've discussed in previous chapters. Regardless of how he got there, it's a tough position to play.

But it works both ways. I could just as easily have been seated on that plane next to a mother-in-law on the warpath, mourning the loss of her son to an undeserving wife. As we've already covered in earlier chapters, some boy mamas find it tough to turn loose. And when the women show up to stake their claim, the MIM feels the vise tighten around his heart.

Survey results fill in some of the blanks. Here's what daughters-in-law told us:

- Nearly 30 percent of DILs were dissatisfied with their husband's level of support when there was a disagreement with his mother.
- Just less than half (49 percent) of DILs thought their husband spent more time with his mother than was healthy.
- Some 53 percent of DILs said they seldom or never see their husband's mother. And 49 percent said that was their preference.

Some of the DILs comments included:

> "It's difficult because my husband likes to please his mom, which upsets me since she has no respect or regard for me."

"It has caused quite a division in my marriage, because my husband would never stand up to her and stand by me to protect me from things she'd do or say. He'd always do what she wanted (such as family events for Christmas, etc.) without talking to me to discuss my plans. I became more resentful, but quietly."

"There were times when she seemed a little possessive of him, and I am totally possessive of my husband. He's mine. I'm sure it put him in a tight spot."

"I want him to stand up for our family to his parents but he won't. I am often left to deal with it."

Moms-in-law had some thoughts to share in the focus groups and survey as well:

"My son doesn't communicate with me. But I still try and reach him anyway."

"We [my son and I] do not have the freedom to communicate as we had in the past."

"We call our son at work, not at the house. They seldom come to family gatherings because she does not like me."

"His new wife has convinced him we shouldn't be friends and has caused great grief in my relationship with my son."

Wives rightfully expect their husbands to defend them from attack and stand up for them when necessary. Moms rightfully expect to have a relationship with their adult sons. Neither are unreasonable expectations. From both sides of the equation, women are in pain. Some are angry, others disillusioned or resentful. Some are simply resigned to the situation as it is. The MIM is caught in the crossfire between two women who love him. If he chooses his wife, it may break his mother's heart. If he chooses his mother, it may destroy his marriage and will break God's heart.

There are two straightforward ways to address this problem. While the MIM has an important role in this process, you can only change yourself. The following tips rely on the action of the two women and set the stage for the MIM to take his responsibility. Ladies first, so let's explore a couple of tips.

Tip #1: Girls! Don't Make Him Choose.

Every man ever born has a mom. She will always be his mom. Wives, you can't change that, no matter how hard you try. Moms, as we've discussed in earlier chapters, your role changes when your son marries. If you expect his world to revolve around you, prepare yourself for heartache. God never intended it to work that way. Each of you has an important role in his life, but the roles are different. If you accept the Word of God as the authority of Christian life, you will see that the roles can and should be compatible, not competitive, as we found with Ruth and Naomi.

We were impressed with the clarity of women's descriptions when answering this question: "Describe your view of an appropriate, healthy in-law relationship. What role would she play in your life, your marriage, your family?" Here are the women's responses; we couldn't improve on their thoughtful answers.

> "There would be mutual respect for one another. We would see each other regularly, pray for each other, and care for each other's needs to some extent. Mostly, I think it's one where the relationship is based on honor and regard for one another. This ties into your expectations for how much time you get with your son, and the freedom for your DIL and son to start building their own life/traditions that might mean less time with them."

> "Respectful, loving, caring. Each knowing our role in the relationship and deciding to live within the boundaries of that role."

"She cares and is willing to share wisdom and advice when asked. She prays for my family daily and is an excellent role model for me and my children."

"My best example would be my sister and her relationship with her mother-in-law. They spend time together and contact each other to share their lives and prayer requests. However, they also have boundaries. Her MIL would not push godly limits with my sister or the rest of the family. She honors my sister's role as the wife of her son. She lives a Christian life worthy of Christ and was willing to provide godly counsel when it was needed and/or requested."

Sounds like paradise, doesn't it? It's possible. It has less to do with how you feel about *her* and more to do with your commitment to honor *Him*. "'Honor your father and mother'—which is the first commandment with a promise—'so that it may go well with you and that you may enjoy long life on the earth'" (Eph. 6:2–3 NIV). It's not a suggestion, it's a commandment, but the promise attached to it is a good one: it will go well with you. And if it's not going well, a long life is just—well, long.

You both love him, that man-in-the-middle. That mutual love should bond you, not tear you apart. Our biggest surprise in the survey was discovering the greatest wound DILs and MILs encountered at the hands of the other. It wasn't the critical MIL commenting that her son's wife was lazy and he could have made a better selection. It wasn't the DIL's claims of the MIL's nosiness, her unwanted advice, or her comments. Nope. The biggest upset was when the other woman was critical of the MIM. When moms hear DILs demean or complain about their sons, they get their backs up quickly. When wives believe their MILs treat their hubbies poorly or disrespectfully, they are immediately upset. Each woman blames the other for the pain experienced by the man in this threesome. It takes two to tango. Why not sit this one out and commit to discussing his shortcomings not with the other woman but with God or a believing friend?

The man-in-the-middle is not completely innocent in this troubling triangle. Many of the stories women shared with us clearly expressed the observation that the MIM found it difficult to speak up when the women in his life struggled to get along. He often disappears completely when they are at war. Failure to take responsibility for leaving and cleaving, as we discussed in chapter 3, is at the heart of tip #2.

Tip #2: Help Him Man Up!

What do the two women in question have in common? The man-in-the-middle. Without him, there is no relationship and no issue. The MIM can and should take action to help establish his household to create a right relationship between his wife and his mother. He should take the lead by setting and communicating appropriate expectations and boundaries. He has scriptural authority to do so. More clearly expressed, it is a mandate from God. But since there are few "leaving and cleaving courses" available, the women in his life can and should help support him in this endeavor. How do you do that?

Tool Kit: Helping Him Become the Man You Both Respect

First, each woman should accept that you have, at times, made it difficult if not impossible for your son/husband to fulfill the leave-and-cleave commandment from God. Ask Him for forgiveness and then ask the MIM for forgiveness as well.

Second, make a decision to support his leadership in following the Lord's direction, and express confidence in his ability to do so.

Third, communicate to your son/husband your desire to fulfill the role God has given you in his life, whether as wife or mother. Let him know you are willing to establish a relationship with the other woman that is based on walking in love with her. Ask for his support and commit to his leadership in the matter.

Fourth, pray for him. Behind every good man is a praying woman, whether it's his wife or his mama, or ideally, both. Ask

God to strengthen him in taking a role that might be new or unfamiliar. Pray aloud the passage from Genesis 2 that introduces the concept of leaving and cleaving:

> The Lord God caused the man to fall into a deep sleep; and while he was sleeping, he took one of the man's ribs and then closed up the place with flesh. Then the Lord God made a woman from the rib he had taken out of the man, and he brought her to the man. The man said,
>
> > "This is now bone of my bones
> > and flesh of my flesh;
> > she shall be called 'woman,'
> > for she was taken out of man."
>
> That is why a man leaves his father and mother and is united to his wife, and they become one flesh. (Gen. 2:21–24 NIV)

It will remind you as you pray for him that it is his call to action as obedience to God. Reading this Scripture passage will remind you to pray for your husband so that he may fulfill this call of action and walk in obedience to God's Word.

Want him to become the man God intended him to be? Most likely, he can't do it without your support and your willingness to let him move from the middle to the lead.

Let's take some time to see how you are doing in this area and where you might want to focus your time and attention. You will find the self-assessment on the next page, and the guided journaling follows.

SELF-ASSESSMENT: Am I Helping the Man Make His Move?

Circle the numbers that best represent the frequency of your behavior for each statement. Use the directions below to determine your score.

BEHAVIORS	Never		Seldom		Occasionally		Frequently
1. I have told the man-in-the-middle to choose between her and me.	7	6	5	4	3	2	1
2. I have not trusted the man-in-the-middle to deal with the issues between my WIL and me, so I have handled it alone.	7	6	5	4	3	2	1
3. I believe it's the MIM's role to help establish the boundaries and relationship between my WIL and me.	1	2	3	4	5	6	7
4. I have put him in the middle on multiple occasions, trying to get him to be the mediator with my WIL.	7	6	5	4	3	2	1
5. I have influenced the MIM to view my WIL in a negative way.	7	6	5	4	3	2	1
6. I willingly submit to God's direction and take the appropriate place (wife or mother) in my MIM's life.	1	2	3	4	5	6	7
7. I have competed with the other woman for his affection and attention because I felt I didn't get my fair share.	7	6	5	4	3	2	1
8. On occasion, I have felt victorious if he sides with me against her and have actively solicited him to do so.	7	6	5	4	3	2	1
9. I have confidence in my husband/son to establish godly boundaries for our family relationships and will accept his leadership.	1	2	3	4	5	6	7
10. I would redirect the MIM back to my WIL if he attempted to complain to me about her.	1	2	3	4	5	6	7

The header also reads: BEHAVIOR FREQUENCY

YOUR SCORE:

Add all the circled numbers. Write the sum in the box:

70–61 Healthy Relationship   40–21 Opportunities for Growth

60–41 Strong Relationship   20–10 Important to Change Behavior

PLAN OF ACTION
Helping the Man-in-the-Middle Make His Move

Review the tips from this chapter as well as your self-assessment score. Use this information to help guide you as you respond to the questions below.

What were the three key points that spoke to your heart in this section?

_____

_____

_____

_____

_____

_____

_____

_____

Stop for a moment and ask the Lord to reveal to you any lessons He desires to add to your understanding.

_____

_____

_____

_____

_____

_____

_____

Write out your action plan.
- WHAT will you do?

_____

_____

_____

_____

_____

_____

_____

_____

- HOW will you do it? (Identify the specific steps.)

- WHEN will you start? (A goal is a dream with a deadline!)

What Would Ruth and Naomi Do?

Since we enter the scene with both Ruth and Naomi already widowed, we don't have a man in the middle of their relationship. But by the story's end, the kinsman-redeemer shows up. Both Ruth and Naomi are eager to please Boaz, and he is accepting of their love and protective of the safety and needs of *both* of the women. The lesson this teaches is clear: everyone is cared for and our needs are met when our relationships are in proper balance.

Prayer

Heavenly Father, please forgive me for the times I have elevated my desire over Your Word and Your will. I accept the role of supporting the man who means so much to me as he moves from the middle to lead his family. I recognize that my behavior may have placed him in a no-win position, whether intentional or not, and I will refrain from doing so in the future. I believe he is called to honor his mother and cleave to his wife and it is possible for him to do both. I will not require him to choose between us, and I will trust him to help support a healthy relationship between the other woman and me. I will request his assistance and counsel if I experience difficulties with her so I may approach her in the most effective way. I will not attempt to influence him to see her negatively. Lord, thank You for establishing the family in a way that is pleasing to You. I accept that Your ways are higher than mine and will submit to Your pattern as the order for my life. *(Inspired by Eph. 5:21–33)*

Chapter 10

Digging Out: How Big Is Your Shovel?

"Does she think my home is filthy?" my mother cried out to my dad. She was heartsick. "I borrowed her pan, and when I returned it, your mother threw it in the trash. She wouldn't think of putting it back into her perfect kitchen! How can she hate me so?"

It was a tense moment for everyone involved, but it had been a long time coming. My father's family (especially his mother) made no secret of their unhappiness when he married outside of his Jewish faith. When Dad let them know his new bride was a Gentile girl, they sat Shiva, a seven-day period of mourning that is observed when someone in the family *dies*. They discontinued all communication with him for several years, considering him dead. Eventually and reluctantly, they relented when my grandfather became ill. Even then, the interactions were difficult, and my mother often felt as though she was merely tolerated and held in contempt by her mother-in-law in particular.

Differences of faith, culture, and ethnicity are a few of the major family hurdles encountered when couples fall in love and marry. But let's not limit the list. Add differing upbringings, personalities, expectations, political parties, and personal style. If it's different, it can be an issue. We are most comfortable with people we perceive are similar to us. Our willingness to trust and be open increases with the familiarity we see and experience in others.

This chapter may not apply to every reader. Many who participated in our survey and focus groups characterized their in-law relationship as good or at least satisfactory. But for others, this was not the case. Often, the primary issue noted was the differences between the two women.

Based on those results, we felt it necessary to address those whose relationships are in bad shape. Some were eager to know what they could do to improve it. Others felt it was beyond repair. Although this may not be your situation, you may know someone struggling with such a relationship. That explained, let's get started.

The Burning Question

**The gap between us is wide. Is it possible to bridge it?
How do I start?**

At this point, you may recognize that there is a big gap between God's expectations for the relationship and what you are experiencing. You may perceive the gap as enormous. Or you may view the relationship as not healthy or God-honoring. Or you may find that it simply lacks the closeness or family feel you had hoped for when you became related. However large that gap may be, if you've accepted God's Word as the authority on the life of the believer, you are ready to address the problem.

On rare occasions, the issue is genuinely one-sided. (Think Jane Fonda in *Monster-in-Law* or Marie Barone in *Everybody Loves Raymond*.) However, our survey revealed that more than 50 percent of women believed they shared the responsibility equally for the status of the relationship. We were surprised at the candor reflected in these numbers. In reality, though, we suspect that the true statistic may be higher. It's hard to see your own share of the difficulty when you are looking so closely at the other woman.

Turning the mirror toward yourself is a good place to start. How different from your WIL are you? What baggage did you bring on this journey? If you have previously experienced wounds in mother/daughter relationships, you may be carrying some of that with you. One of our survey respondents wrote, "My mother-in-law has a poor relationship with her own daughter. There's been rebellion and a lot of hurt. My MIL would love for them to be close, but that ship has sailed—it's never going to happen. They are so different, and my sister-in-law has turned from her faith. I realize that much of the mama anger is not about me. It's helped me to recognize that."

Even if you didn't throw the first punch, have you continued to keep the fire burning? It may be an active or passive process. You waded in and gave what you got: that's an active process. Or you withdrew from direct combat and kept the situation alive by talking about it with anyone who would listen: that would be passive.

Awareness of your role in creating the problem may be dawning, or you may believe sincerely that your hands are clean. At this point, it doesn't matter. If the relationship is in trouble, God asks us to step out and prepare to do His will and His work. It's not about who did what or who's to blame. It's about accepting responsibility to walk in love. Each of us is responsible for our own behavior; God is responsible for the results when we are obedient to walk according to His will.

First Thessalonians advises us to dress properly in the Spirit: "Since we belong to the day, let us be sober, putting on faith and love as a breastplate, and the hope of salvation as a helmet" (1 Thess. 5:8 NIV). Joyce Meyer puts it like this: "How do you put on something *spiritually*? You have to plan for it *mentally*." We must plan ahead of time to

- Compliment and encourage
- Forgive quickly
- Bless those who curse us
- Focus on the needs of others

In other words, don't wait for the feeling to kick in to foster a change in your approach. Feelings are fleeting and subject to change. Plan kindness. The way you put on love is to decide to love unconditionally and then follow through.

I can hear some of you asking, "So I'm supposed to be pleasant in the face of her punishing attitude? Slap on kindness along with my favorite shade of lipstick?" Yes, you've got it!

Paul continues in his instruction to the Thessalonians: "Make sure that nobody pays back wrong for wrong, but always strive to do what is good for each other and for everyone else" (1 Thess. 5:15 NIV).

What makes this difficult is our own pride. Humility is the antidote.

> A gentle answer turns away wrath, but a harsh word stirs up anger. (Prov. 15:1 NIV)

> Pride brings a person low, but the lowly in spirit gain honor. (Prov. 29:23 NIV)

> As a prisoner for the Lord, then, I urge you to live a life worthy of the calling you have received. Be completely humble and gentle; be patient, bearing with one another in love. Make every effort to keep the unity of the Spirit through the bond of peace. (Eph. 4:1–3 NIV)

God requires humility *and* He empowers it: "But he gives us more grace. That is why Scripture says: 'God opposes the proud but shows favor to the humble'" (James 4:6 NIV).

You are not required to submerge all your feelings, desires, preferences, and needs in order to do things your WIL's way. Taking a humble stance does not mean that you should let her disrespect, control, or manipulate you for her own selfish ends. You may need to establish appropriate boundaries, which we will discuss in the next chapter. What it does mean is that you will choose your own behavior. You will respond with the love of God and not let her choose your behavior, causing you to react, returning evil for evil.

Sound tough? I'm not going to lie, it's not easy, and Jesus knows it. He embodied humility. "In your relationships with one another, have the same mindset as Christ Jesus: Who, being in very nature God, did not consider equality with God something to be used to his own advantage; rather, he made himself nothing by taking the very nature of a servant, being made in human likeness. And being found in appearance as a man, he humbled himself by becoming obedient to death—even death on a cross!" (Phil. 2:5–8 NIV).

Some of our respondents shared their success in making this verse their personal commitment:

> "She has caused me great pain, but over the years God has shown me I need to forgive her for all those things and forget about them. Life is too short to dwell on the negatives, and I am thankful for all the positives He has given me through her."

> "As I walk in love and forgiveness, I try to think of how I want my children to treat me. God continues to open my eyes as to how I can love more and stop judging and criticizing her."

When our own sons married, we reminded them to be clear that the family experiences they had become accustomed to in our home worked for *us* as a family. We cautioned them that their brides would come with their own set of experiences. We encouraged them to be open to finding the best of both worlds, discarding what didn't work for them as a couple. We also suggested they look beyond their combined experiences. The challenge comes when we see *different* and judge it as *wrong*. Different is not wrong. It's simply different, but often we do not understand the difference.

Finding the pan in the trash can was a difficult moment for my mother. She felt judged and rejected. Mom's translation, however, of her mother-in-law's intention was faulty, limited by her lack of full understanding regarding the rules of a kosher home.

"When you asked to borrow the pan, do you remember what she said to you?" my dad asked.

"She told me to keep it. But I told her that I just wanted to borrow it and would return in on our next visit."

"Honey," he said gently. "She keeps a kosher kitchen. There are rules and regulations about how to do that correctly. Once the pan left her home and was no longer treated according to those rules, she couldn't bring it back into her kitchen. She cares about you so much that she'd rather give you the pan than insult you with the explanation."

When we fail to understand, we fill in the blank with our own interpretation:

- She hates me.
- I'm not good enough (and never will be).
- I'm just his mother and no longer important in his life.
- Keep your mouth shut. Your advice is worthless (and so are you).
- I'm a bad wife, mother, homemaker, cook, etc.

Once we have filled in the blank with our personal (but inaccurate) translation, we live as though those words came from her mouth. We may even believe she actually said them. Once offended, we may return fire and the battle rages.

Making an attempt to understand her will bring answers. I married an only son, his mom's favorite child, so say his sisters. He was and will always be special to her. Did I see her as a bit overprotective when we dated? Perhaps. She spent time getting to know me. She asked me questions about my life, my faith, and my interests. At times, it felt like an interview—or even an interrogation. It often left me feeling a bit unsteady.

Years later, she acknowledged her tactics. "Ron was called to be the head of his home," she said. "I knew that would only be possible if the woman he married supported him in following God's plan and *allowed* him to lead." It wasn't that she didn't like me; it was her desire to see her son walk in God's direction with a godly partner by his side. What mother wouldn't want that?

How do you get started? The tip sheet, self-assessment, and guided journaling pages await you.

TIP SHEET
Making a Fresh Start

For Your Eyes Only

- Complete the self-assessment on the next page and identify patterns or trends you see that are beneficial to the relationship and also any that are not. Include them in your Action Plan.

- Ask the Lord to reveal any past wounds or hurts unrelated to your WIL relationship that have crept into your baggage. Identify the differences that may be an issue. Ask God for healing in those areas, so that you are able to set them apart from your WIL relationship.

- Ask the Lord to forgive you for your role in making the relationship difficult. Be specific about behavior that has not been godly. Confess and commit to leaving those behaviors behind.

Scripture Reading and Study

- Spend time creating a list of Scriptures that will support your new behaviors. Start with a word search to include *humility*, *grace*, *pride*, and *forgiveness*.

- Read the four chapters of the book of Ruth and, for each of the two women, make a list of characteristics that stand out to you as important. Don't hurry through this. Take your time. The differences between Ruth and Naomi were many; review how they dealt with them.

For Her Benefit

- Pray for the other woman every day. What are her needs? Her fears? Her concerns? Her hopes and dreams? Lift them before God and ask for His blessings on the relationship.

- Drop her a note via social media, text, e-mail, or U.S. Mail to share things about her that you appreciate or admire. Don't overdo it—once every few weeks is sufficient.

For the Man You Both Love

Let him know about your decision to live in peace with the other woman. Ask for his prayers and support. Ask his forgiveness and share with him your commitment to unite the family, walking in love and alignment with the Word of God in this relationship.

SELF-ASSESSMENT: Digging Out—Is It Worth the Effort?

Circle the numbers that best represent the strength of your belief about each statement. Use the directions below to determine your score.

BELIEFS	Strongly Disagree		Disagree		Somewhat Agree		Strongly Agree
1. I understand and accept that "different" is not wrong.	1	2	3	4	5	6	7
2. Pride has kept me from reaching out to the other woman, even when I know my behavior was hurtful.	7	6	5	4	3	2	1
3. I do not believe the relationship will improve.	7	6	5	4	3	2	1
4. I am committed to demonstrating Christ's love for the other woman and praying for her regularly.	1	2	3	4	5	6	7
5. The status of the relationship is not my responsibility, because she is the one who is difficult.	7	6	5	4	3	2	1
6. Our differences can become a strength rather than a weakness, and I am open to exploring new ways to positively accent our differences.	1	2	3	4	5	6	7
7. There have been times when I've used the other woman as an excuse for my own behavior, such as anger or unkindness.	7	6	5	4	3	2	1
8. I believe it's possible to influence her behavior by ensuring I remain calm and behave in a kind and respectful manner.	1	2	3	4	5	6	7
9. I don't think she's capable of a good relationship with me.	7	6	5	4	3	2	1
10. I accept that the Word of God requires me to respond with love rather than return evil for evil, even when I've been wronged.	1	2	3	4	5	6	7

YOUR SCORE:
Add all the circled numbers. Write the sum in the box:

70–61 Healthy Relationship   40–21 Opportunities for Growth
60–41 Strong Relationship   20–10 Important to Change Behavior

PLAN OF ACTION
Digging Out: Starting Fresh!

Review the tips from this chapter, as well as your self-assessment score. Use this information to help guide you as you respond to the questions below.

What three key points spoke to your heart in this section? What are some areas where you and your WIL are different that you may have judged as her doing it wrong?

_____

_____

_____

_____

_____

_____

_____

_____

Stop for a moment and ask the Lord to reveal to you any lessons He desires to add to your understanding.

_____

_____

_____

_____

_____

_____

_____

_____

Write out your action plan.
- WHAT will you do?

_____

_____

_____

_____

_____

_____

- HOW will you do it? (Identify the specific steps.)

_____

_____

_____

_____

_____

_____

_____

_____

_____

_____

_____

- WHEN will you start? (A goal is a dream with a deadline!)

_____

_____

_____

What Would Ruth and Naomi Do?

Jewish custom required Naomi to provide new sons for Ruth and Orpah to take as husbands, but that was impossible. And Ruth (or Orpah) needed to provide Naomi with a child from that family bloodline to count as her own—basically their version of Social Security. But there seemed to be no way.

Just when Ruth and Naomi felt stuck with no escape, God provided the answer. The women created a fresh start because they were willing to step out of their past and seize a new opportunity—the journey to Naomi's homeland. There, they followed after Jehovah God. Once they were in the right place (symbolic of being in the right place spiritually), the answer was right in front of them: Boaz, the kinsman-redeemer. When we think there is no way out of our impossible situation with our WIL, that the gap is too great and the hole is too deep, God will provide an answer for us too.

Prayer

Heavenly Father, I thank You for opening my understanding to the possibility of a fresh start with my WIL. I recognize that I am accountable to You for the behavior I choose. Please help me set aside pride and choose humility in my relationship with her. I look to Jesus as my example of building integrity and relationships through humility. I recognize that my WIL may not immediately return the effort, but I commit to aligning my choices with Your Word. I accept that I don't have to feel like blessing others in order to do so, as feelings aren't reliable. Remind me to plan kindness. I will put on love by deciding to walk in love and following through. I will love when it's easy and when it's not, because You abide in me and empower me to offer grace as I have received it. *(Inspired by Phil. 2)*

Chapter 11

Good Fences Make Good Neighbors: Setting Boundaries

*S*he came for a week and stayed a month. I was worn out and angry by the time she finally left," Alison said. "She never asked if she could extend her visit. She just didn't leave. I wanted my husband to address it with her, but he said he wasn't comfortable doing it. Well, big deal, buddy! I wasn't comfortable with her here. She's in my face, under my skin, and overstaying her welcome." Alison continued, "If it had been my mother, you can bet he would have found his voice, comfortable or not."

Setting boundaries can be challenging, but they also establish clarity that can make life easier for everyone involved. Alison felt as though she were living in occupied territory. As she explains, "It's my house, and she seems to forget that. She knows how I feel about smoking, and I'm sure she thinks I can't smell it when she's in her room. She's wrong. She cleaned out cupboards when I was at work, throwing away things I wanted, and even rearranged the furniture. I feel as though we're under siege. The kids started asking, 'When's Grandma going home?'"

Most of us would consider this MIL outlandish, thoughtless, and rude. When we observe actions way past the bounds of good taste like this, we may think, "Who raised her—wolves?"

How we were raised is a good place to start understanding the situation. Our past experiences may differ widely from our WIL's. We didn't have the same parents; our guidance about what is acceptable behavior varies. And as we've examined in earlier chapters, those differences can create real problems for everyone involved. If that person is our WIL, there is trouble brewing for us both.

Boundaries are defined as limits, borders, or restrictions. God established many boundaries and restrictions for His people in the Old Testament. One example is the dietary rules set for the Israelites. These laws determined what they could and could not eat and even how to prepare the food. They weren't arbitrary; they were designed to protect the health of His people.

The Burning Question

What are personal boundaries, and do I need to set some?

When we feel our health (emotional or physical) is endangered, personal boundaries can help. We can create boundaries by setting safe, acceptable limits and permissible ways for others to behave around us. This also allows them to understand what to expect when those boundaries are not respected.

Boundaries are built out of a mix of beliefs, opinions, attitudes, past experiences, and social learning. In other words, you have a personal rule book. So does your WIL. Want to bet they're not the same? Sometimes we drop hints when we detect a rule violation. Sometimes we blow up. Neither approach is successful—at least not on a permanent basis.

If you need guidelines, rules, or limits to protect yourself, your family, your home, or your sanity, setting boundaries should be on your to-do list.

How do you draw the line without making an enemy? In what areas should you establish guidelines? Let's take a look at some tips and strategies.

Your Home

Your home is your turf—your domain. Is smoking allowed in your home? Is it okay to bring alcohol to a party in your home? What are the expectations for children when they visit your home? Can they jump on the furniture or run through the house screaming? Do closed doors send the message "Do not enter"? You have the right to set the standard for behavior in your own home. You are also responsible to communicate your boundaries to others who spend time there and not expect them to read your mind.

Alison's mother-in-law in our opening story made assumptions about how long she would be welcome as a houseguest in her DIL's home. Why not? Most likely it had never been discussed. Her own experience may have led her to believe that family is *always* welcome. Alison may have been raised with the axiom, "Houseguests, like fish, begin to stink after three days." In her MIL's mind, cleaning out the cupboards was helping out, lending a hand. To Alison, it felt like a terrible violation of her privacy. Prior to the MIL's visit, if Alison would have spelled out her expectations using the SPEAK communication tools found in chapter 7, it would have helped both women enjoy a better visit. Using that format, here's how it might sound in a pre-visit phone call:

"Hi Mom. I'm looking forward to your visit next month. I'd like to fill you in a bit so you are comfortable with our routine. Things can be a bit crazy at times with the kids' schedules, and with my work hours as well as Tom's. Do you have a few minutes to talk about our time together?

"I want to make sure I have the dates of your visit right. Arriving on the fourth and departing on the eleventh, right? That's a nice long visit, and it works well for us. The following week, Tom will be traveling, and I have a major project presentation at work, so the week you've chosen is perfect. I know you're aware that Tom and I prefer you not to smoke in the house. The deck is screened in, and I'll make sure there are ashtrays available for you out there. The weather is supposed to be beautiful.

"Tom and I both have to work a few days of your visit. He works Monday and Tuesday, then the rest of the week is open. I have to work Tuesday and Wednesday, so we'll each have some time with you to ourselves, which will be nice. I want you to be on vacation during your visit. No cooking, no cleaning—just relax and enjoy yourself!

"What else can I share with you about our schedules or our time together? What can I get from the grocery store that you would enjoy? I want to make sure I have it on hand. Are there any activities or places you'd like to go during the week you are here?

"Please let me know if anything comes up. The kids are excited to see Grandma. Talk to you soon."

It's not a forceful conversation. If there was a conflict last time she visited, you may need to be even more direct, using the SPEAK method. Remember, tone of voice and expression (if face-to-face) all count. Your home is your castle, and you want your WIL to be comfortable when she's there. You deserve to be comfortable as well.

Your Children

My hubby and I once enjoyed a wonderful weekend away that was enabled by my MIL's willingness to babysit our four-year-old while we were gone. On our return, he eagerly told us about all the things he had done and proudly displayed a gift his nana had bought him in our absence—a bag of green plastic Army men. It appeared to be an entire regiment, battle-ready. On closer inspection, it was obvious these were Special Forces. Knowing that we did not allow our son to play with guns but not wanting to disappoint her grandson, my mother-in-law had painstakingly cut every weapon—gun, grenade, and knife— from the hands of the battalion.

The experience was both funny and touching all at the same time. It's important to say that she did not agree with our no-guns policy. She pointed out that her son/my husband had played with more than his share of war toys as a child with no adverse effect. Even so, she respected the boundary we had communicated as to how we would raise our son. Our confidence in leaving our boys with her grew because we knew she would support our choices.

What are your boundaries? No soda or caffeine? Limits on sugary treats? Meals are always eaten at the table? No PG-rated movies for your third grader? These are your decisions to make on behalf of your children. You are responsible for them, which includes safety, health, and so much more. We had good friends who told our sons, "Oh, you can call me Julie." We don't believe seven-year-olds should call adults by their first name, so for close friends, Miss Julie or Mr. Michael was acceptable to us. We communicated this guideline to the kids *and* to our friends, who then helped us reinforce our belief by reminding the boys when they slipped. They became partners with us in the process of raising our sons.

The T-shirt that says, "What happens at Grandma's house, stays at Grandma's house," is shorthand for "When the kids are with me, I will do what *I* think is best. Your rules do not apply here." I'm not fond of the sentiment and it can be problematic, but it's good to remember the boundaries you set are not the Ten Commandments. They don't have to be written in stone, but they shouldn't be an Etch-A-Sketch deal, either. An occasional scoop of ice cream at grandma's house before bed is not a disaster. Be reasonable and balanced. SPEAK is a solid tool to address breaches in the process if they become a concern.

Finances

"The way to get along with my DIL is a simple formula," claimed one survey respondent. "Keep your mouth shut and your checkbook open." Whoa, that's cold, but it does happen. How do you avoid becoming an ATM for your son and his family?

"My in-laws helped us with the down payment on our home. Now they think they're entitled to make comments on everything we buy." Janelle sounded angry. "They criticized the car we bought, calling it a luxury car. They're always mentioning we eat out too much and could save by eating at home. I'm sick of it. I wish we'd never accepted their offer of help!"

Many young couples struggle with money, particularly early in their marriage. Sometimes the issue is not enough income.

Sometimes there are differences of opinion between husband and wife about spending or saving habits. And at times, the young couple may have expensive tastes on a small budget. They can support themselves, but it may not be the lifestyle to which they'd like to become accustomed.

The media reports many young adults in their mid twenties believe they are deserving of the same standard of living as their fifty-year-old parents: the big house, the new SUV, the exotic vacations. And many parents are helping to support that expectation by becoming their adult children's savings and loan, or worse yet, their ATM.

Establishing boundaries around finances is important for the parents-in-law as well as the young couple. As the senior in-laws, you've worked for your money; you've saved or invested wisely. You are entitled to choose how you manage your finances without feeling guilty or manipulated to support your children's desire to live above their means. So a word to the wise for the young married couple: if you and your husband rely on his parents' ready reserve, you may find your lifestyle under the microscope.

One of the financial boundaries we established in our own family precluded cosigning on a vehicle loan for any of our children. "If the bank thinks you can't pay it back on your current income and denies your loan request, they're probably right. We don't want to see you get in over your head. A new car would be nice, but it looks as though a pre-owned vehicle is in your future." Our thoughts on this issue were clearly communicated from the time the boys had their driver's licenses. It wasn't always popular, but it protected all of us and prevented conflict.

Circumstances of an unusual nature such as the sudden loss of a job or an illness that drains emergency funds may prompt a different response. You will be best served to prayerfully consider any request for financial help. If your boundaries are clear and have been observed in the past, this may be one of those exceptions-to-the-rule moments. Again, boundaries must be

Good Fences Make Good Neighbors: Setting Boundaries

flexible to meet unique situations. Check with God. Let Him help make the final determination.

A quick word to the MILs: come to an agreement with your husband on this issue. He may be viewed as the hardliner and you as the soft touch. If you secretly distribute cash with the reminder, "Don't tell your father," you have broken agreement with your husband and endangered your own marriage.

If you are approached for financial assistance, never agree to give a gift or loan without discussing it with your spouse and submitting it to God in prayer. Let your kids know you love them and will do what you believe is right in the Lord. Help them to understand if your answer is no by SPEAKing in love, using the tools in chapter 7.

Your Emotional, Mental, or Physical Health

Up till now, we have discussed boundaries based on your preferences. But sometimes the potential for genuine danger requires boundaries at a much higher level.

"One of my husband's earliest memories is of his mother chasing his dad with a knife she took from the kitchen," Kendra told us. "When she's upset she can become unstable and unreasonable. She has a mental illness that she refuses to deal with. We have chosen to limit our time with her—and she is never alone with our children."

"If I upset my DIL, even over something small, she will retaliate against me," Laura said. "If I can't babysit when she asks me to, or if I've gone to the mall with my other DIL and she wasn't included, she gets angry. Her favorite way to punish me is to tell me I can't see the baby. That used to hurt me terribly, but I've gotten used to it. She'll call again when she needs something, and she'll act as though the two months apart had never happened." Laura has accepted the behavior, and while she misses the time with her granddaughter, she has decided she will no longer cry and try to win back her daughter-in-law's good graces when these events occur.

"My DIL, Roseanne, is abusive. She bullies me, calls me

terrible names, and uses unforgivable profanity." Marjorie fell silent for a moment during our interview, twisting the tissue in her lap. "My husband and I have addressed it with her and our son, Roger. Roseanne never does it in from of him, and she always denies it. But others in the family have witnessed it. At first, I tried to talk with her, to let her know I was not willing to be treated so poorly, but it had no effect on her behavior. As a result, I have discontinued my relationship with Roseanne entirely; it's just too painful, and if I'm honest, I must admit I'm afraid of her and I worry for my grandkids. My son brings them to our home when he visits, but we are never together for holidays or birthdays. My heart is broken. I do think Roger believes me, although he has never said so."

These were among some of the saddest of our interview conversations. These women have come to a difficult conclusion: life with their WIL is not a healthy choice. They have established boundaries that either limit interactions or terminate contact entirely. None of the women made these decisions lightly. They prayed and sought counsel, some with mental health professionals. Is it the right thing to do?

No one need accept abuse of any type. You are entitled to protect yourself and your family. Like Marjorie, such a decision should be bathed in prayer and the counsel of godly friends, your pastor, or professionals.

While your relationship with the man-in-the-middle will most likely be impacted, he may decide to continue the relationship with your WIL on his own, as we saw with Roger and his mother, Marjorie. This may be difficult to accept, but it is important to remember that he, too, has a relationship with the other woman. If she is his mother, that was his first and perhaps most intimate relationship he had with a woman until he married. If she is his wife, he has a responsibility to the marriage and to his family. Be careful about issuing an ultimatum that forces him to choose between the two of you. He is entitled to both his wife and his mother.

The boundaries we have discussed—children, home, financial, emotional, and so forth—just scratch the surface. There are many Christian books available on the importance of boundaries in families, with insights to help you establish limits that will best serve all parties. If you find yourself in a situation similar to those we have discussed, I urge you to visit your nearest Christian bookstore and access the resources available.

One last, important suggestion: pray for your woman-in-law. Your heart will become soft and pliable as you stand in prayer for her, and that will help you tune in to the Lord's direction in dealing with her.

Let's take a quick assessment to determine whether you need to set some boundaries to regain your balance.

SELF-ASSESSMENT: Have We Lost Our Balance?

Circle the numbers that best represent your agreement with each statement. Use the directions below to determine your score.

	BEHAVIOR FREQUENCY						
BEHAVIORS	Never		Seldom		Occasionally		Frequently
1. I usually bite my tongue when my WIL oversteps her bounds in words or deeds.	7	6	5	4	3	2	1
2. We are dependent on my MIL to help us with finances on a regular basis. —OR— My son and his wife are dependent on our financial help on a regular basis.	7	6	5	4	3	2	1
3. I am comfortable addressing my WIL when I believe her behavior is rude or transgresses my personal preferences in areas like my home or the way she communicates with me.	1	2	3	4	5	6	7
4. If I am unable to say something nice, I say nothing at all.	1	2	3	4	5	6	7
5. I have punished my WIL in some way when she has upset me or made me angry. I think she got what she deserved.	7	6	5	4	3	2	1
6. I am uncomfortable with my WIL's behavior. I have suggested to the MIM (or others) that she may need professional attention.	7	6	5	4	3	2	1
7. My WIL and I disagree on how to raise children, and she believes I don't do it correctly.	7	6	5	4	3	2	1
8. I believe I am responsible to make my WIL feel comfortable in my home, but not at the expense of my values or beliefs.	1	2	3	4	5	6	7
9. My WIL's behavior is erratic and often aggressive, to the point that I am no longer comfortable in her presence.	7	6	5	4	3	2	1
10. I am committed to the boundaries we have established and am unwilling to be flexible on any of these areas. There are no exceptions to the rules.	7	6	5	4	3	2	1

YOUR SCORE:
Add all the circled numbers. Write the sum in the box: ☐

70–61 Healthy Relationship
60–41 Strong Relationship
40–21 Opportunities for Growth
20–10 Important to Change Behavior

PLAN OF ACTION
Boundaries Create Balance!

Review the tips from this chapter as well as your self-assessment score. Use this information to help guide you as you respond to the questions below.

What three key points spoke to your heart in this section? What boundaries do you need to set?

_____

_____

_____

_____

_____

_____

_____

_____

_____

Stop for a moment and ask the Lord to reveal to you any lessons He desires to add to your understanding.

_____

_____

_____

_____

_____

_____

Write out your action plan.
- WHAT will you do?

_____

_____

_____

_____

_____

- HOW will you do it? (Identify the specific steps.)

_____

_____

_____

_____

_____

_____

_____

_____

_____

_____

_____

- WHEN will you start? (A goal is a dream with a deadline!)

_____

_____

_____

What Would Ruth and Naomi Do?

There isn't a specific example from the book of Ruth that can help us know exactly how Ruth and Naomi would go about making and honoring boundaries with each other. There is, however, an important lesson to learn: there is a big difference between walls and boundaries. We witness Naomi's bitterness as a way to process her grief. This becomes a wall attempting to hold others at a distance: "Go back to your mother's house." Not only did it keep people away, it caused her to die a little bit inside. Walls will cause our hearts to become bitter. Fortunately, Naomi needed Ruth so much that she let her inside the barrier even though her bitterness was certain to be off-putting for Ruth. We make relationships difficult when we either don't have any boundaries or have too many boundaries.

Prayer

Heavenly Father, I ask for Your guidance as I assess where I need to establish boundaries with my woman-in-law. Please show me the areas where my expectations are reasonable as well as areas where I need to relax a bit and be more flexible. Guard my heart as I watch over what You've called me to protect. I desire to use the boundaries to allow my WIL and me to better understand and meet expectations, not to keep her out of my life.

Give me courage to address the areas I have ignored, and help me to do it in a way that strengthens our relationship. I will honor the boundaries my WIL has made clear in her communication with me, and I pray she will do the same with mine. If there are areas where I believe my family or I are exposed to emotional, mental, or physical danger, I ask that You give me the wisdom I need and lead me to the resources (books, ministerial support, professional counseling) that will help me understand my WIL while protecting myself and my family. I trust in You for the peace You give to guard my heart—a peace that surpasses anything I can figure out on my own. *(Inspired by Prov. 4:23; Phil. 4:7; James 1:15)*

Chapter 12

Well Begun Is Half Done: Starting Strong

*M*om, I'm bringing Dari home to meet you and Dad. I'm so excited! You are going to love him, I just know you will!" Kimberley's voice said more than just the words themselves; Kim's mother, Donna, knew her daughter had fallen in love.

Donna recounted that phone call as she shared the news of her daughter's recent wedding and the story of their engagement. Kimberly, nearly thirty, is an only child and close to both her mom and dad. She is one of those "everything you could have hoped for" girls.

Donna and her husband, Dan, looked forward to the visit. They were certain the relationship was serious from information Kimberly had shared with them. Even though Dari was born and raised through his teen years in Lebanon, they were unconcerned about the cultural differences and ready to meet him with open hearts.

Donna and her husband welcomed Dari, and both were eager to make him comfortable in their home. They worked hard to get to know him in the short three days the young couple visited. Although Dari was a bit on the quiet side, everyone seemed to enjoy the visit. Donna was excited when Kim dropped a hint or two about marriage. The issue of the differences in their faith came up briefly. Kimberly assured her parents she would never waiver in her relationship with Christ. She shared privately with them that Dari was not religious, and should they decide to marry, she would continue to follow her own faith, as would their children.

Donna and her husband were not surprised when Dari

phoned two months later, asking for her hand in marriage. Dari confirmed Kim's assurance that there would be no pressure for Kim to convert to his religion, and he expressed respect for her Christian beliefs, letting Dan know he had even attended church with Kim on a couple of occasions. Christians had been present in Lebanon for ages, and he was certain it would not be an issue with his family. Satisfied with the discussion, Donna's husband gave his blessing.

The first hint that things might become complicated came early in the wedding planning. Dari's parents insisted on paying for the event, explaining that in their culture, it is the responsibility of the groom's family. As the financiers of the wedding, however, they felt entitled to express strong opinions on the wedding arrangements. The couple had chosen a beach wedding with a civil ceremony. Dari's family was not happy with their decision. His mother pressured the young couple to reconsider, but they were resistant. Donna and Dan would have preferred a church wedding but felt the couple had the right to create the experience that suited them.

The pressure from Dari's family to incorporate religious and cultural elements into the big day became a daily discussion, and Kimberly was often the target of her soon-to-be mother-in-law's campaign. Dari, also an only child, was the light of his mother's life, and although she seemed to accept Kim, she made it clear she would have preferred a bride of the same faith. Dari steered clear of the conversations whenever possible and asked Kimberly to deal with the details. The conversations were often tense and had on one occasion ended with her future mother-in-law angry and Kimberly in tears.

The campaign extended to the engagement party, the bridal shower, and every facet of the wedding. Kimberly was certain she loved Dari; she wasn't certain she would ever feel the same way about his family. Dari eventually suggested they offer an olive branch and include some of his mother's requests, assuring Kim it would help pave the way for a better relationship between the two women.

The couple did make some concessions, more than Kim preferred. What should have been a joyful time became an endurance contest instead. Donna, her husband, and even the bride and groom were glad when it was all over. Dari and Kim were relieved and were anxious to move on with their life together as husband and wife without future family issues.

What do you think? Are they in the clear?

This couple had unwittingly set a precedent and didn't even realize it. But Dari's Mama did. She was successful in the wedding plan push, and now she feels motivated to continue, with great persistence, to advise the couple on a variety of subjects: finances, job opportunities, timing of having a first baby, and more. She may see her uninvited counsel as helpful, but it feels a lot like meddling to Kim and Dari. Neither is happy about it, but Dari has managed to stay above the fray, and it often falls on Kim to field the calls from her MIL.

If you are engaged, pay close attention: the time between the proposal and saying "I do" is an extremely important period. There's vital work to do, and we're not talking about choosing china patterns and centerpieces. It's time to establish the standard for your lives together and be clear with both families. *The leaving and cleaving begins now.*

Make your choices and create your big day the way you and your groom want it to be while honoring both of your families, including their cultures—if and as appropriate. If you and your groom allow yourselves to be bought, pressured, guilted, or manipulated into the wedding of either mama's dreams, you are on a slippery slope. You are establishing a precedent that includes unsolicited advice and pressure on how you will raise your kids, spend your money, celebrate the holidays, and where and how you live.

Taking your stand is much more difficult if parents on either side are footing the wedding bill. The family that pays may believe they are entitled to have more decision-making power. As a couple, you must decide whether that is a consequence you are willing to accept. Whether you are or whether you decide to pay your own way, the goal is to have a day that honors God and your union and to still be on speaking terms with both families once the rice is swept away.

🔥

The Burning Question

How do we initiate the leaving and cleaving process, plan a wedding, and still maintain good relationships with our families?

It may not be easy, but *it is* possible. Here are some tips and ideas for starting strong.

Tip #1: Honor the Role Your Parents Have in Your Lives

As soon as you become engaged, invite *both* sets of parents, if possible, to a dinner with the purpose of honoring them and their investment in your lives. Acknowledge it was their guidance, counsel, and support that helped the two of you grow to maturity. Thank them for their help in preparing you to take the step of marriage, where you are no longer dependent on them, but instead, will now rely on God and your spouse.

Share the Scripture from Genesis 2 and pledge your commitment to always honor them while acknowledging that the relationship is about to undergo a major change. Help them understand the significance of leaving and cleaving if they are not familiar with the concept, and ask for their support as the two of you move together, unified in marriage and in your desire to do it as God has commanded.

Ask them to pray with you on this occasion and to pray for you as a couple throughout the wedding planning as well as throughout your married life. Ask each parent to share one important marriage lesson they could pass on to you.

A gift might be a nice touch to commemorate the event and

will help formalize this break from "in my parents' care" to "standing with my spouse, together before God."

Tip #2: Set and Clarify Expectations

You've dreamed about your wedding day for many years, most likely. Believe it or not, your folks have probably also imagined what this day would be like. But there's a strong possibility that your dreams and theirs are not identical. When expectations are unmet, hurt and upset emerge. To prevent that, now is the time to discuss details and address any assumptions or expectations. Some questions about the wedding plans to cover include:

Finances

Who will pay for what? How will financial decisions be made? What expectations come with the financier's investment? In other words, if your families are paying, will they expect to be involved in all decisions or have ultimate control or veto power? Is that acceptable, or do you need to renegotiate that expectation?

Establishing a wedding budget from the beginning may be a great way to sidestep the need for approval on every decision. For example, budgeting no more than *x* amount on the venue or *x* amount on the music or flowers will help satisfy the need to influence, but you and your groom will still be able to select the location or flowers you prefer within that agreed-upon budget. If that does not appeal to you, perhaps you and your groom should consider financing the big day on your own, even if it means making simpler plans.

Please remember, the wedding is one day in your life; the marriage is to last a lifetime. I've often shaken my head at the elaborate and expensive weddings I've attended for marriages that lasted less than a year. The focus and preparation was on the wedding, not the marriage. How much time are you and your fiancé investing in preparing for your life together? Keeping things in balance with the proper perspective may help when you start to believe that you cannot live without the imported peonies from France in your bouquet.

Cultural/Religious Observances

If there are differences in culture, ethnicity, or religion, will they be observed and included in your big day? If so, how? Discuss your preferences with both families and identify ways to honor family and cultural traditions in a way that is acceptable to you and your groom.

I once attended a wedding that featured both bagpipes and a mariachi band! Different, yes, but a fun way to acknowledge the mixed heritage of the couple and the families present. It might not be what you had in mind, but look for ways to include touches that represent each of you and the heritages you are bringing to the marriage.

Differences in faith can be much more difficult to handle. If you are reading this book, my hope is that you and your groom share Christ in common. Your families may not. Discuss with them your beliefs and the spiritual foundations on which you will build your lives. It may still be possible to have an ecumenical approach to the ceremony itself. I've known of Christians who loved the idea of "jumping the broom"—an early tradition born of African-American wedding customs. A Hebrew Christian friend chose to incorporate the *chuppah*, or canopy, featured at Jewish weddings. It made her parents' dreams come true without violating any of her own beliefs.

Honoring dissimilar backgrounds may not be easy to do, but it is usually possible. Just as the wedding symbolizes the union of a bride and groom who come from different cultures, the ceremony can incorporate symbols representing these different backgrounds. If the marriage is considered doable (despite different backgrounds), then combining cultures in the wedding should be doable too! One guideline we suggest is that you make it clear that you will not incorporate anything into the ceremony that would transgress your commitment to Christ or in any way compromise the beautiful message you have the opportunity to send about your faith on your wedding day.

Family Involvement

Choosing your honor attendant might seem like a no-brainer to you. Of course she will be your college roommate, best friend from high school, or a colleague who has become a confidante. But is there a sister who might be upset or angry about your choice? What if the groom's only female cousin felt she should have been included in the bridal party? Is your sister expecting her two-year-old son to be the ring bearer, but you and your intended had decided on using his German shepherd to walk it up the aisle? Again, expectations not discussed can lead to bad feelings down the line.

Who will be involved? How will it be communicated? Discuss the families' expectations about their roles. I felt very left out of a family wedding when everyone, including some close friends, was given tasks and invited to help—except me. When I expressed my hurt after the wedding (in a rather pouty way, I'll admit), the bride was surprised to learn that I had wanted to assist, since my schedule had been ridiculously crazy. She was being thoughtful; I was acting immaturely.

Make the choices that reflect the day you and your intended desire. Take into consideration family relationships and expectations as you plan. And communicate your decisions early, so all family members are clear.

People who love you are happy for you and anxious to support you in a meaningful way. Let people invest in your day if possible, and remember that such investments are an expression of their love. Someone has to oversee the guest book (the pen hander-outer is important!), greet guests as they arrive at the reception while you are still taking photos, or help your elderly aunt pin on her corsage and get from the ceremony site to the reception.

You are off to a solid start! Use the tools from chapter 7 to communicate effectively and from chapter 6 to resolve conflicts, should any arise. You are doing the right thing according to the Word of God and are establishing precedents for your life with your husband-to-be. It's work, but it's worth it. The wedding magazines will tell you exactly what's in fashion for your day, but they won't tell you how important the preparation process is in establishing the leaving and cleaving principle. Don't delay! Gain understanding about your situation before you set any more plans in motion. The self-assessment and guided journaling are a step in that direction. They are found on the next few pages.

SELF-ASSESSMENT: Are We Starting Strong?

Circle the numbers that best represent your agreement with each statement. Use the directions below to determine your score.

BEHAVIOR FREQUENCY

BEHAVIORS	Strongly Disagree		Disagree		Somewhat Agree		Strongly Agree
1. My fiancé and I have discussed our wedding plans and are in agreement as to what we want the day to be like.	1	2	3	4	5	6	7
2. Family is providing finances for our wedding. We established a budget and are staying within it.	1	2	3	4	5	6	7
3. Family members who want to be more involved in decision making for the wedding are pressuring us.	7	6	5	4	3	2	1
4. We have communicated with our parents about the principles of leaving and cleaving.	1	2	3	4	5	6	7
5. There has been conflict between the two families about the wedding plans.	7	6	5	4	3	2	1
6. My fiancé and I do not agree about some of the wedding arrangements.	7	6	5	4	3	2	1
7. There have been times when I've contemplated eloping to avoid the conflict brewing about wedding plans.	7	6	5	4	3	2	1
8. We are preparing for marriage through pre-marital counseling with our pastor or other professional.	1	2	3	4	5	6	7
9. We have discussed our plans for dealing with cultural, ethnic, or religious differences with our families.	1	2	3	4	5	6	7
10. We believe our wedding is an opportunity to share our commitment to Christ visibly and plan to do so.	1	2	3	4	5	6	7

YOUR SCORE:
Add all the circled numbers. Write the sum in the box:

70–61 Healthy Relationship   40–21 Opportunities for Growth
60–41 Strong Relationship   20–10 Important to Change Behavior

PLAN OF ACTION
Starting Out Strong!

Review the tips from this chapter as well as your self-assessment score. Use this information to help guide you as you respond to the questions below.

What were the three key points that spoke to your heart in this section?

_____

_____

_____

_____

_____

_____

_____

_____

Stop for a moment and ask the Lord to reveal to you any lessons He desires to add to your understanding.

_____

_____

_____

_____

_____

_____

Write out your action plan.
- WHAT will you do?

_____

_____

_____

_____

_____

_____

_____

_____

- HOW will you do it? (Identify the specific steps.)

_____

_____

_____

_____

_____

_____

_____

_____

_____

_____

_____

_____

_____

_____

- WHEN will you start? (A goal is a dream with a deadline!)

_____

_____

_____

What Would Ruth and Naomi Do?

We aren't sure how Ruth's marriage to Elimelek started out, but we do know she started her marriage to Boaz on better spiritual ground than was present in her first marriage. Naomi's sons married women outside their faith system. This is never a good foundation for marriage, but because of their circumstances, they made do. Many believe Ruth converted from her Moabite religion to embrace the Jewish faith. In Ruth 1:16, Ruth tells Naomi, "Your God will be my God." By the time she married Boaz, she was prepared for the best way to enter into a faith-filled marriage.

Prayer

Heavenly Father, I ask for Your guidance as we plan our upcoming wedding. I understand that while it is an important day, it is just one day out of my life. I recognize that I may be tempted to focus on the details of the wedding and, as a result, spend less time preparing for married life. I commit to making our lives together my focus.

I recognize that it is important for us to establish ourselves as an independent, unified couple during this engagement period and to set clear expectations with our families. Help us to honor our parents in this process while initiating the principles You have established for marriage. These principles primarily involve leaving our parents and cleaving to one another. Remind us that we are setting precedents as we plan for our wedding that will either work for us or against us in the future. Help us communicate with our parents and other family members with care and concern, help us preserve and nourish our family relationship, and most of all help us honor You in the way we enter this life together as husband and wife. *(Inspired by Rom. 12:1–18)*

About the Author

Deb DeArmond is wife to her high school sweetheart, Ron—who showed her the path to becoming a Christ-follower thirty-eight years ago—and mom to three incredible sons. She is also Gigi to three perfect grandboys. But Jesus is her favorite, and the guys have learned to live with it. She is a transplanted Californian who has been a proud Texan for almost nine years, and she loves the Lone Star state!

Living her midlife optimistically, Deb feels excited to experience what comes next and what God has for her now. She longs to see women find their passion and place in the body of Christ, show up, and finish strong. One of Deb's favorite quotes comes from author Agatha Christie, who said, "I have enjoyed greatly the second blooming. . . . Suddenly you find—at the age of fifty, say—that a whole new life has opened before you."

Deb loves to cook, write, and spend time with her family, whom she considers to be the best evidence that God loves her. Traveling is a passion, and she has been fortunate to visit all fifty states and six foreign countries.

An entrepreneur, Deb has owned her own leadership training and coaching practice for fifteen years. She is also an experienced speaker on topics that include family, relationships, communication, and conflict. Deb serves as a featured writer for two online magazines, *Living Better After 50+* and *Destiny in Bloom*, and is the cofounder of My Purpose Now (http://mypurposenow.org).

Connect with Deb at Deb DeArmond: Family Matters
debdearmond.com